THE WILD HUNTERS

GENE CAESAR

The Wild Hunters

THE WOLVES, THE BEARS
AND THE BIG CATS

G. P. Putnam's Sons   New York

© 1957 by Gene Caesar

*Published on the same day in the Dominion
of Canada by Thomas Allen, Ltd., Toronto.*

Library of Congress Catalog Card Number: 57-11712

MANUFACTURED IN THE UNITED STATES OF AMERICA

VAN REES PRESS • NEW YORK

This book is affectionately dedicated to
Beauwood Rocky, A. K. C. H-389070,
whose penetration of the mysteries of the wild,
I'm certain, has been far deeper than my own.

THE AUTHOR wishes to thank Dick Johnston and Reginald Wells of *Sports Illustrated*, Ted Kesting and Zack Taylor of *Sports Afield*, Alden Norton of *Argosy* and *Adventure*, Noah Sarlat of *Sportsman*, *Sport Life* and *Hunting Adventures*, Ray Robinson of *Real*, and George Murphy of *True Adventures* for their kind permission to include in this book experiences, incidents and other material which he first described in article form in their respective publications.

CONTENTS

INTRODUCTION

THE ANIMALS described in this book are carnivora or predators. Like men, they eat the flesh of other animals.

Most of these creatures face extinction within the next fifty years. The generations to come will find them only in textbooks and museums.

A few of the wild hunters will be slaughtered for the ornamental value of their hides. Some will be killed off because they fight the advance of civilization so cleverly, thieving and destroying. But the great majority of these animals are being ruthlessly exterminated simply because they are predators. In other words, these animals are being driven over the brink of extinction under the guise of saving other animals.

It is true that several of these creatures will readily prey on livestock. There is no doubt that a few of these animals have, on extremely rare occasions, attacked and even killed human beings. I have no quarrel with those who insist that civilization and the nature of the big predators are incompatible and that civilization must come first. As a human being I have to accept as axiomatic the law that civilization must come first, although some other human being will have to explain why.

My argument is with those who seem to believe sincerely we must destroy the timber wolf to save the caribou or destroy the puma to save the deer. I sometimes wonder if these men cling to the remnants of mythology and consider all carnivora except man to be creations of evil forces in the universe. Believe me, the same Power that made the lamb made the lion. And nothing was created without a purpose.

Once there were only the wild creatures on the face of this continent. The land was clean and green. The forests had never been cut nor the rivers polluted. The grasses grew with the movement of water in the earth through the circling of the seasons. The caribou and elk, deer and buffalo and moose followed the grasses. The wolves, the bears and the big cats followed the grass-eaters. The wild things flourished together in the years before man.

Why were predators necessary? If a herd of grass-eaters grew too large for the browse, starvation threatened them all. But predators always swarmed to the area where their prey was the thickest, reduced oversize herds to a level that could survive. What purpose of Nature did wolves fulfill when they followed the buffalo? The main defense of the herd lay in its speed. The slow aged bulls were pulled down and the fertility of the species was kept at a high level. The sickly animals were easily overtaken and epidemics were prevented.

These aspects of the scheme of Nature, considered more fully in the chapters that follow, are usually referred to as biotic checks and balances. Somehow, they seem to be too profoundly simple for the human mind to fathom. Men are perfectly capable of understanding why nations must build huge armies to prevent war, why a large national debt means prosperity and why there will be more food for everyone if the government pays the farmers to let the land lie fallow. But it seems impossible to convince the very great majority of people that a certain amount of predation will mean larger game herds.

A few self-styled naturalists of the "mechanical" school will doubtlessly accuse me of "anthropomorphizing" the wild hunters. This means endowing them with qualities that only human beings actually possess. It has become quite the fashion lately for men who live in laboratories to experiment a few hours with beetles and bugs, then write very long books insisting that their findings prove that such things as bravery, loyalty and mother love belong strictly to human beings and that the observations of centuries of natural history are pure nonsense.

There is little need to credit a wild animal with human attributes. For his needs, for survival in the world he knows throughout the life he leads, his own are superior. The average predator is a far more skillful hunter than any Boone and Crockett Club record-holder. The wild things know hunger and cold, just as we do, but they also know an endurance, a will to stay alive, that is rare among men. There is a degree of patience known only in the wild, possessed only by creatures that hunt and kill as a means of life, which surpasses human understanding. The ability to wait motionless for hours and then pounce, the ability to stalk as slowly as the minute hand of a clock moves— this is self-control never possessed by man.

A wolf family, pulling down an elk or caribou, exhibits teamwork that would belittle the efforts of our best athletes. And the bond of affection and loyalty that exists between members of that family would shame a great many families in the world of men. The wild hunters can feel approaching changes in weather and prepare for them. They have a sense of direction that is beyond the range of our understanding.

No, there is little need to endow wild things with human characteristics. In spite of the blood-chilling accounts written by those who consider predators to be creations of the Prince of Darkness, the beasts of prey do not kill for amusement, as we do. The patriarchs of a wolf clan do not show their courage by sending their sons out to die, as we do.

Why anthropomorphize any animal when the qualities they already possess defy the humble limitations of human understanding? The greatest of our scientists today cannot begin to explain the magic that takes place in the nose of a beagle as it chases a rabbit.

I vaguely remember an old story in which a man finds himself in a vast meeting hall, filled with every living creature on this earth. The fate of the human race is to be decided and he is to be the spokesman. Unless two other animals will speak for man, *homo sapiens* will go extinct. The dog speaks for him immediately and stands beside him. But the horse runs off laughing. The cat haughtily refuses because he asked the dog first. One by one, the wild creatures give their opinions of us. At the last moment, when everything seems lost, a thin lonely voice comes to the rescue. The mosquito speaks for man, too.

In speaking for the wild hunters, I'm not trying to escape my share of the guilt inherent in our ruthless domination of this globe. Like the mosquito, I'm merely being selfish. I want to see those tracks in snow, hear those calls on winter nights for many years to come. I want the knowledge, when I hike through the forest, that the possibility of glimpsing one of these fascinating exemplars of the laws that shaped the universe still exists.

GENE CAESAR

Ann Arbor, Michigan

BOOK ONE The Wolves

I

THE WOLF'S POINT OF VIEW

THE little hunting and fishing village of Jordantown had never before seen so many big cars. Nor so many big men. A well-known wolf-hunters' association had descended on our town that afternoon. Nine cars and a dog truck crowded our street. Twenty-six strangers filled the Spikehorn all through the evening.

"I still can't see what you need me for," I told the tall man in red woolens. "You people have your own dogs. And your own way of hunting. I..."

"Hell, you know the country," the man said. "We don't skimp on anything. We don't take any chances. We sure have got our own way of hunting. And it's perfect if I ever heard of it. It's the one sure way of guaranteeing you get a wolf. You go out with this 'copter-pilot Reynolds got hold of, as soon as it gets light. Check all those little islands east of here. Can you tell wolf tracks from the air?"

I nodded.

"And you should know the best places to try, living up here. As soon as you find an island with tracks leading in and no tracks leading out, you have the pilot call back here. We drive down along the ice and spread out around that island. When everybody's ready, Simmons puts the dogs on the line. They rout the devil out and somebody's sure to get him. It's perfect. We can't miss."

I sat in silence over my drink and looked at the men around me. Men of wealth, I realized, men of importance and position who journeyed hundreds of miles in their long expensive cars and paid fantastic amounts of money for these brief escapes from the pressures of their lives.

"Run through that again," the man beside me was saying to the tall hunter. "This is new to me. We just make sure he's in there and then surround him, huh?"

"That's it. The pilot'll take off the minute it's light enough to see. The dogs Simmons got this time were blooded on wolves out West. They'll drive him out. With us spread out, maybe a hundred yards apart, there'll be no missing him. He won't have a chance."

I nodded my head slowly. The tall man was right, the wolf wouldn't have a chance. It most certainly wasn't hunting. Whatever it was, as the man had put it, it was perfect.

"The way we hunt a wolf track means a wolf hide. We get them."

I nodded again. The man on the other side of me, the camera-carrying man, introduced himself. He was a member of the Outdoor Writers' Association and he was fat and likable.

"I'm neutral," he told me. "I want to get the wolf's side of

18

the story, too." Then he laughed. "But I mean it. How does he feel, what does he think about when ..."

"How about it?" the tall man interrupted him. "You want the job? You going out with the pilot tomorrow?"

"Yeah," I told him. "I can't refuse that. It's easy money."

"I still wonder how the wolf feels about all this," the camera-carrying man was saying.

The tall man laughed and I had to smile a little.

"I've never asked one," I told him.

The wolf that prowled the forest that skirted our town that night had never heard of werewolves. He did not know that since the unrecorded years his kind has been a symbol of all that is evil and terrible to mankind. He only knew that he had never, since his puppy days, gone without being hungry. And so he hunted.

Through a bitter night he worked the thickest cover in a ten-mile circle, prowling with cold and silence and loneliness. But the forest lay adamant. No scent could be detected in the frost. Nothing moved.

Then, in the hour before the false dawn, he found the large blobs of a white hare track, dotted through the pines, miles long in the search for food. With the night nearly gone the wolf trailed swiftly, forcing his tired muscles through the deep snow.

But hope drained away. The trail led to the frozen shore of the lake and on across toward a small island a few hundred yards out. The wolf searched the shoreline in both directions and found nothing. The hare was still on the island. The wolf waited in the thicket. In a full night of hunting he had not broken cover. Every instinct told him not to cross the ice.

Hunger and fear balanced themselves within him as he waited. But hunger was the determinant, the force behind all movement of wild things on the wild land. Hunger seemed a great void inside him as he waited in the deep snow. And when he closed his eyes, it was as though he floated in that void, swaying and dizzy. He knew that if he went through the day without food he might be too weak to hunt the next night. Hunger was stronger than fear.

The wolf made his decision, then stepped at once through the thicket into the open. He waited for several seconds. Nothing happened. Then he trotted swiftly but carefully over the smooth ice, his legs slipping, the hardness of the surface jarring the bones of his shoulders.

The wolf, at mid-morning, knew only that something very, very unusual was taking place. And the unknown meant danger. Fear lay beside him in the cedar thicket.

He had killed his hare at daylight, trailing nearly to the center of the island, slowing as the scent strengthened, finally slithering on his belly over the snow, inch by inch, then throwing all of his strength into a leap for the fern clump. A quick shake of his jaws and another of the little things that ran and quailed on the wild land had died in silence. And he'd had food until the next night.

He had stalked his hare, but daylight had stalked him, and even in the thickest cover he now felt naked. He thought of the long stretch of open ice he had to cross, of the road on the other side of the swamp, and the cold dread bit him more deeply than the icy wind on the lake. His hills seemed very far away.

When the helicopter had come suddenly from the sky, swung along the shoreline, then darted down and hovered between the island and the shore, the wolf had dodged back into the cedars. Now the craft rested on the ice and he watched and waited silently.

Something was going on along the road beyond the far swamp. Only the wolf's eyes moved as he searched for the occasional movement of a car on the road. He knew cars. He even knew planes, although this one on the ice was strange to him. The wolf knew many things. He had crossed concrete roads in his life, loped under spans of power lines, slipped beneath fences. He knew men and feared them. But he held even greater fear and hatred for their dogs. He had been hunted before.

But it came. Somewhere in the swamp the excited bugle of a hound challenged him. Fear bit into every inch of his hide, every bone of his body. Fear was a deeper, more maddening pain, now, than hunger had been. The urge to run twisted inside him.

He rose without a sound, backtracked almost to the place where he'd killed the hare, then leaped suddenly off the trail to a snow-covered deadfall. He balanced himself for a second, then ran the length of the log and sprang far into the snow. He moved back out to the edge of the cover, farther away from the place where he'd entered, and then waited, watching the ice.

There were now many men and four hounds. The wolf watched them steadily, all of his hatred burning in his yellow eyes. Three of the hounds were blueticks, old and grizzled. The fourth was a young lean black hound who somehow seemed more excited, more eager than the others. The wolf's eyes singled him out, focused their hatred upon him. And he waited.

He saw the dogs held in leash just ahead of the plane. But the men were spreading out around the island. The wolf had never been hunted in this manner and he sensed a new danger. He growled softly to himself as one of the men took the position just ahead of him on the ice. The terrible fear that the wild thing has of the trap shuddered over him. The sweet cold patience of the wild was no longer with him. He wanted to run, to charge the dogs and fight. He knew he must merely remain hidden now.

He knew nothing of death so he could not really be afraid of it. He knew all about cold, all about hunger, all about fear. He knew what it meant to be alive. And as he lay there, a wild animal in a trap, he had one feeling—he wanted to live.

Hound voices exploded on the ice to his left and all of the pent-up fear broke loose in him. He tried to flatten himself deeper into the ferns. He fought the instinct that told him to run.

Hound voices moved into the island, the bugling of the small black hound moving out ahead of the bawl and chop voices of the other three. The wolf heard them cover each detail of the stalk he'd made that morning, then the kill. He heard the bugling of the black hound pass the deadfall where he'd lain before, then cut out and wail the loss. Still the wolf had to wait.

The blueticks had none of the impatience of the black hound. The wolf heard them brushing against the thick cedars as they worked over the loss in silence. Then a single bawl and chop voice sounded the discovery of the last trail he had left. The wolf doubled his legs beneath him.

The young black hound took the lead again, his unearthly bugle splitting the air. Then the wolf could see him, the dark shape weaving quickly through the cedars. He waited until the dog was actually upon him.

Then he sprang up, his giant gray shape dwarfing the hound. As the dog crashed into him, the wolf's curved yellow teeth slashed savagely, opening the black hide from the ear to the shoulder. The hound screamed with pain and turned to run. The wolf made a quick bound, slashed and then held. The hind legs in his teeth ripped sideways and the black hound lay kicking in the snow.

He felt teeth sink into his hide. The blueticks were upon him. He slashed back at once, but his teeth would not send the older dogs running. The blueticks would fight until they were killed. Somehow, he knew this.

He crashed into another hound, fang against fang, shoulder against shoulder, fought his way past and bolted into the thick brush toward the far end of the island. He broke through the cover, noisy and reckless, frantic to put a breathing space between him and the hounds. He was willing to fight them for his life, but a fight in one spot would bring men. He knew that. The hound voices thundered behind him.

He reached the island's edge, hesitated, then stepped boldly from the cover to the ice and waited. Ice exploded at his feet with the sound of a shot and he sprang back for the thicket, quartering off for the lake side of the island just as hounds came through to the point where he'd broken cover.

There were no men on the lake side of the island. He ran along the ice, hugging the shore cover, circling the island to his right. The other shore could not be seen. Miles of smooth bare ice lay to his left. The hounds were on the ice behind him now, working steadily, close together. He bounded uneasily along the shore, his nails digging in as his legs slid.

He rounded the point. A man was there on the ice. The wolf jumped for cover again just as something stung one of his haunches and buckshot rained into the thicket. Numb with despair, he felt no pain. As he ran for the center of the island he heard the three hounds break into the thicket behind him.

At the deepest section of the cover he turned and waited. He was going to fight now. Men were everywhere between him and his hills. There was nothing else to do. He crouched and waited as the three blueticks hurried toward him, their terrible determination ringing clear in their voices.

He sprang to meet them. Even in the denseness they circled to fight him, three ugly fight-wise old blueticks. Each time he lunged at one, to smash shoulder against shoulder, another was at his flank.

Finally he caught one against a tree-trunk, ripped its neck open, tore its ears, but the teeth of the other two forced him to dodge back and the fallen hound rose again to fight. There were new noises in the brush to one side, then the sound of a rifle. The men were here now.

As abruptly as he had made his decision to fight, he made his decision to run. He dodged through the cedars, headed directly for the hills, and he gave no thought to the sounds around him, had no fear of the open ice ahead. He only knew that he was going to run as long as he had life and strength left.

He bore straight onto the ice. All his strength, every muscle in his body, was concentrated on his running. And he had a thought as he ran. He was going to make it. He was going to live. Men were still shooting at him. He had the swamp ahead

23

and then a road to cross, ridge after ridge to climb. Hounds were behind him. At least two of them would follow until he either lost them or killed them. But, somehow, he knew that he was going to make it.

His legs drove firmly beneath him, again and again and again.

I stood at the edge of the cedars and watched the wolf's dash for the swamp, as the concentrated fire of a half-dozen rifles spurted the ice about him. I did not fire my rifle. I had used it only once, to end the suffering of the young black hound. As I watched the wolf now I realized that the animal had broken cover directly in front of the stand I had left when I went to stop the hound's tortured screaming. And I didn't care, I didn't care who knew about it.

It was really something, I told myself, *really something*.

The fat man was suddenly beside me, his camera in his gloved hands.

"He made it!" The man was laughing. "That gray devil made it. And you know something? I'm glad. I really am. He didn't have a chance. He didn't have a chance in a million."

"Yeah," I said. Two blueticks were crossing the ice now and men were following. "If they let the hounds run that fellow up into the hills, they'll never come out again."

"Yeah?" the man said. "Well, you see what I was talking about before? What did the wolf think? How did he feel during this whole deal? That's what I'd like to know."

I watched the man for a minute. "Afraid," I told him. "Afraid and hungry. Wild things are always hungry. And always afraid."

The man looked at me strangely and I turned away. "If Simmons wants tar for that other hound's neck, I've got it at the house." I started back across the ice.

A week, a month from then ... maybe I'd feel like hunting another wolf. But if I did, I'd take my scoped Remington and my two slow, cold-nosed black and tans and start into the hills on a cold track. I'd hunt as the wolf hunted. I'd know the silence, the cold and the loneliness of primitive country. Above all, I'd know the wonderful patience of the wild.

Just then, I wanted to get to the Spikehorn quickly. I had a bad taste in my mouth.

II

THE FIGHT AT TOKLAT RIVER

THE big female wolf watched and waited. She was very worried. Fear grated along the bones of her body. She lay tight to the earth in a hillside thicket. From time to time she turned from her watch on the ground above and looked toward the hills that rose in the north. But each time she saw nothing and snapped her head back to stare at the slope and the coming danger.

Her mate had gone alone into those hills the night before to hunt. Now mid-morning was bright. The Alaskan summer sun was warming the ridges. And he had not returned. A sickening fear had grown steadily inside her throughout the morning. For this was the north country, the land just below the barrens, where predators and men compete savagely for caribou meat, where strychnine and cyanide and traplines and airplanes are matched constantly against wild strength, wild cunning and the age-old skill of the hunter.

Two young gray-black wolves lay beside her, scenting her fear and knowing their own. They had hunted beside their parents for two winters and they knew fear just as they knew cold and hunger. For two years they had learned the lessons of keeping alive and they understood what it might mean if their father did not come back from a night's hunt. They had drunk a fear in their mother's milk. Since the days when their parents had fed them by gorging themselves on caribou meat and then returning to throw up the chewed flesh before the den, they had lived with apprehension and dread. They knew how new snow

26

can conceal a trap, how a kill might be poisoned when they returned to feed. They knew the distant crack of a rifle and death coming suddenly with nothing near, no creature to fight for their lives. They knew these things well because they had once been part of a much larger litter.

When daylight had crept into the thicket, they'd left the den in the swale below, the new-born pups crying after them, and had gone up on the ridge top to keep watch with their mother. Hour after hour, as they waited with no signs of their father, the cold dread had increased within them. Then suddenly this new danger had appeared above them. And fear had exploded inside them. They too watched steadily now, their lips drawn back over curved yellow fangs.

Far up on the slope, four giant grizzlies were moving, moving with a gait that was at once ponderous and cat-like. And their gait marked them for what they were—the most ferocious of bears. They were not aimlessly wandering, not grubbing out the deadfalls and bushes of the hillside. They were going somewhere, moving in a straight line, a line that would take them within a few yards of the wolf den. And they would pass downwind. As always, at whelping time, a huge quantity of meat was buried in the growth beneath the den. The huge grizzlies would never pass without scenting that cache. And they came on, closer and closer.

The affection and loyalty that exists between members of a wolf family are unique in the animal world, paralleled perhaps only by human beings. The two young wolves waiting beside their mother in the thicket knew that they could live through the summer months ahead by hunting for themselves. But they also knew that the new pups could not, that the stored meat was the only hope for this spring's litter. There was no question in their minds as the powerful, savage creatures many times their size came on down the slope. No matter how terrible their fear, they lay still, watched their mother and waited.

The big brown female wolf had been hoping against the mounting pressure of anxiety that the four shaggy giants would change the direction of their travel, turn either up into the hills or down toward the river. But now the grizzlies were little more than a hundred yards away. The hope was gone. Even if they turned, now, the scent of the cached meat would reach them. She would be forced to fight. The only decision left was when to attack. She snarled soundlessly.

She wanted her mate back, back where he belonged when dawn bared the cover and the hunting hours were done. His place at whelping time was here on the ridge top. Hers was in the den below where the helpless pups were whining now and wondering.

The grizzlies came on, their shambling pace never slowing. Suddenly the leader, the largest of the four, stopped and reared high on its hind legs, dwarfing the bushes and scrub saplings. His powerful forepaws dangled limply, the massive head turned slowly from side to side, drinking in the thick liquid scent of aging meat.

All of the grizzlies were standing erect now, forty yards away. The mother wolf watched, her teeth bared, her snarl choked back. Bears had never looked bigger. Moving through sparse cover, trampling through stunted trees and short hillside bushes, their size made them seem out of place in this country, giants in a normal world. One by one they dropped back on all fours and started upwind, straight toward the swale that hid the den.

The two-year-olds waited for their mother to pick her moment. She remained frozen against the earth, staring tightly. Now the nearest grizzly was no more than thirty feet from the den mouth.

In a silent, lightning-fast rush, the three wolves attacked.

The leading bear, moving eagerly toward the enticing promise of a feast, reared up again as the three shapes came out of no where, ripping into him, slashing from both sides. He recovered his balance and fought back with his great paws flailing in deadly, smashing strokes. But he swung at empty air. The wolves had gone by, attacking each of the grizzlies and dodging out of reach.

28

The bear reared up again as the three shapes came out of nowhere, ripping into him.

They turned and raced back through the brush, wheeling in and slashing again, never still, knowing well what one blow from a grizzly's club-like paws could do, knowing that their chances lay entirely with their speed. Again and again they slashed and ran, slashed and ran.

The sweeping attack carried back along the file of bears, then threw its full weight against the grizzly nearest the den. The mother wolf leaped straight at his face, crashed against him with her fangs raking. She dodged back out of reach, then stood her ground, a sharp yelping battle cry beginning to sound in her throat.

The giant bear swung forward, bore down to crush and destroy this creature one fifth his size that so absurdly dared face him. But both of the young wolves were at his back, their jaws clamped like vises on his haunches, their teeth sinking deep. With a great roar the grizzly turned and struck. But the two-year-olds dashed out of reach and the mother wolf was on him again.

The big bears had filed toward the thicket expecting to feed, not to fight. The surprise of the wolves' sudden and frantic attack confused and unnerved them. All at once they turned their backs and bolted, up past the den, out of the thicket to the open slope. The wolves stayed at their heels, ripping and tearing into them from behind. The sharp, broken yelps of a chase cry rang out steadily now.

In the open the grizzlies stopped and turned on their tormentors, bunching tightly together while the wolves stormed around them. Massive beasts that they were, they had none of the wolves' quick nervous sensitivity. Confusion and surprise were merging into anger within them. But this came about slowly. And while the advantage of the sudden attack was still with the wolves, they carried the fight.

It is true that the strength of the wolf is the pack. No human athlete could even remotely conceive of a team as perfect as this one that now played a game of life and death. The mother wolf would challenge a grizzly, moving in very close but never too close, sometimes even feigning a crippled leg to get the bear to start after her. The split second that he lunged forward and separated himself from the other grizzlies, one of the young wolves would be ripping at his haunches, tearing desperately at the heavy hide to get through and cut a tendon. No matter how quickly the bear turned and struck, the wolf would be gone and another would be at his back. Only when the grizzlies bunched tightly together were they safe. The instant one of them started to bear down on a wolf, he was surrounded by three raging furies of fang and claw that were never still.

But in the minds of the shaggy giants the numbing surprise was melting, anger and battle-cunning were brimming more and more fully. Their movements became faster, their eyes sharper. Their confidence surged back and more than one of them began singling out a wolf for attack at the same time. Their grating bawling roars came steadily now, dimming out the frantic yelps of the wolves. The bears were just becoming aroused, were just really beginning to fight.

The mother wolf saw the change and threw all of her speed, strength and skill against it. She took more chances, came in faster and farther, sank her fangs deeper and stayed longer. Grizzly jaws closed like rifle shots beside her head. Bear paws caught her glancing blows as she darted away, flipping her through the air and sending her tumbling, but always she whipped to her feet again, kept moving and slashing.

The mother wolf had wanted nothing more than to drive the bears beyond the range of the cached-meat scent, then turn back to guard her den. But the ridge top where the hungry grizzlies made their stand was far too close. As her fight became frantic a paralyzing despair was coming over her. Battling these giants was very much like matching fang and claw against wind or mountains or a winter's cold. Grizzly hide was simply too thick, the vital spots too well protected. The fight raged on and on and there was no gain, no giving of ground.

But there is a strength of patience known only on the wild land, known only to creatures that hunt for their livings. The self-control that enables a lynx to take hours in stalking a few feet closer to a wary snowshoe hare before pouncing, the ability of a coyote to wait motionless on its belly in a thicket while grouse moved closer—this patience belonged to the wolves. They had sometimes spent days in pulling a caribou bull away from the herd or trapping a sheep below the safety of its rocky peaks. And now, as they fought a dangerous battle with no gain, as rush after rush failed to drive the grizzlies from the ridge, there was no thought of slowing or stopping. They had lived by patience. They had learned to trust it.

The fight swayed back and forth in the open, mounting to its fullest frenzy now as the bears took the initiative. Suddenly the mother wolf realized that the struggle had carried back until the invaders were on the very edge of the den thicket. The two-year-olds followed at once as she changed her way of fighting. Now she tried only to lure the grizzlies back up the ridge, keeping them faced above, cutting between them and the brush, lying as if stunned to draw them after her.

But it was too late. One of the bears was in the swale now, ripping away the earth that covered the cached meat. All three wolves threw their weight against him, kept their teeth in him, but the bear went on after the meat, almost as unconcerned as though they were bees guarding a honey tree he'd decided to rob. In a quick rush all four of the grizzlies broke into the thicket, trampling over the den entrance itself.

The time for skilled fighting, for slashing and dodging, was gone. The mother wolf bounded to the den, turned and bared her teeth. She heard her pups crying behind her. And this time, when a bear pounced on her with his full weight and the terrible strength behind his claws, she stood her ground.

The great bulk smashed her against the earth and half-smothered her, but her legs were never still, her jaws constantly snapping. She was lifted, held clear of the ground in a deadly grip. She felt life going from her as she fought, kicking and screaming, twisting like a hooked trout. Fang against fang she raked at the bear's mouth as he tried to bite down on her.

She knew she was going to die now and it was as much against death itself that she fought as against the monstrous animal that held her. Death was a thing unknown and the unknown meant fear. Life was constant hunger and cold, but life was also the feel of her pups beneath her, the exultant thrill of a chase, the taste of a fresh kill. And she wanted very much to live. Tooth and claw fought the grizzly. But every nerve in her body and every bit of her will fought death.

All at once she felt herself being dropped to the ground. The big bear fell back and rolled over, pain shrilling the pitch of his roar as he tried to stand. The two-year-olds had attacked from behind, fighting just as savagely as though they themselves were held in the bear's grip. One of them had finally chewed through to a tendon.

The useless leg hung limp as the grizzly backed away from the wolves, but the others were still in the thicket, still unearthing the buried meat. The young wolves carried on the fight without hesitation, rushing the bears repeatedly, trying to separate and cripple another. The mother wolf rose again to the battle, but now, as she slashed and dodged, she kept herself always between the grizzlies and the den, ready to stand her ground once more if a bear got too close to her pups.

The struggle was deadlocked. The invaders had broken into the stored meat but they could not feed. Their claws and jaws had to be ready at all times as the wolves kept up the attack with no evident limit to their endurance. But the bears could not be driven from the thicket. Each new frenzied rush seemed to only increase their determination to drive off their tormentors until they were left alone with the hoard of buried meat. Even the crippled grizzly stood his ground, sitting back in the brush, his mighty arms flailing with all their deadliness.

For another hour the fight by the den raged on. Every twig in the thicket was broken and painted with blood. The reddened ground had been torn apart in the search for meat and every one of the wild creatures that moved through that nightmare setting, unreal in bright sunlight, was bleeding from a dozen wounds.

Then, little by little, the battle started to slow. Very nearly three hours had passed since the big female wolf had first led the attack down the ridge, and through all that time the wolves had been constantly moving and never slowing. But now the mother wolf was not leading the fight. Fearful of leaving the mouth of the den, she fought only a quick darting battle on one side of the swale. The two-year-olds were actually carrying the brunt of the fight by themselves now and the hopelessness of their attempts was wearing them out. More and more they paused to rest before each new rush. And now the grizzlies were finding time to gulp a few mouthfuls of meat before having to whip around and smash at quick, sharp-fanged shadows. The deep-throated roars and the yelping cries were no longer a steady, even medley. The fight was broken now by ominous stretches of silence.

It was during one of these lulls that a faint sound came from the hills in the north. The wolves hesitated, their ears lifted and alert, then suddenly threw themselves at the invading giants with new strength and courage. Even above the sounds of the renewed battle, the sharp yelping chase cry came steadily from those hills—nearer and nearer, louder and louder.

The father wolf was back.

He was a huge gray wolf, a creature that feared nothing but man, a lord among wild things. When he threw back his head and howled in the night or when his chase call rang clear in the air, the forest went dead quiet, the game trembled in the thickets. And now, even as they fought off the new viciousness of the attack, the grizzlies turned their heads to watch the ground above as that terrrible cry came out of the hills.

A blurred gray streak shot into sight on the ridge, bounded down the slope and leaped into the thicket without slowing. One hundred and fifty pounds of muscled fury drove fully ten feet through the air to crash against one of the shaggy giants. The bear lost his balance and went down with the ripping, snarling

34

terror sending great horrible slashes across his arms and face. They rolled back to their feet, still locked together in a deadly tangle, then broke apart. And this time it was the bear that dodged away. As soon as his legs hit the ground the big male wolf threw himself straight at the throat of another bear.

There was no standing before him, this hurricane of anger that whirled about recklessly in a fever of destruction. He bounded about in the midst of the grizzlies, tearing and rending, in constant and terrible motion that defied the size and strength of the bears, the deadliness of their heavy-muscled, long-clawed arms. He seemed a creature gone mad, a creature that knew nothing beyond the slashing use of his jaws.

The grizzlies fell back, away from the den and the swale. But even in the open the wolves raged about them. Once more the element of surprise lay with the wolves and they carried the advantage to its fullest. The two-year-olds seemed to gather new speed and daring from their father's frenzied, unceasing example. The mother wolf was still in the struggle, but even now she kept herself between the bears and the den.

The grizzlies had had enough. They were trying to leave but the wolves seemed to be on all sides of them. The male wolf had wisely singled out the crippled bear, striving with each rush to finish him off, forcing the others to ring tightly about him.

All at once the grizzlies turned their backs on their enemies and bolted down toward the river. The three wolves kept up their punishing attack for another hundred yards, raking the heavily-furred haunches again and again. Then, as if a signal had been given, they turned back to where the mother wolf waited.

They stood together for a long time before the den. Then the big gray wolf trotted to the ridge top and looked out over the hillside growth to the river. The giant bears were still in sight, moving away slowly with the crippled one falling slightly behind.

The male wolf came back down to the swale. The battle he had just won for his family had been no gentlemanly duel, no

35

affair of honor. It had been fought over meat. And hunger was the determinant, the moving force behind nearly everything that took place on the wild land. Mercy was a thing as unknown to him as it was to his enemies, whether animal or human.

Winning wasn't quite enough.

If he harassed the bear pack long enough, he knew, kept at their heels with the patience and persistence that was life itself, they'd eventually leave the cripple behind. In a very simple and direct way, the grizzlies would repay that which they'd stolen.

He started down toward the river, in no particular hurry now. One of the two-year-olds followed after him.

The mother wolf watched for a few seconds, then turned and snaked her way into the den. The clamor of the new pups rose to a higher pitch, then quieted into a murmur of soft, contented sounds.

The other two-year-old wolf walked up through the growth to the ridge, then settled down out of sight in the brush to watch and wait.

III

THE LAW OF THE BARRENS

In the gray bleakness of dawn on a day in September, a large herd of barren-ground caribou moved slowly across the flat tundra of Alaska. The great southward migration, in which they would march in a line a dozen animals wide and a mile long, had not yet begun. They wandered in small bunches now and fed on the lichens. Their winter coats were well-developed and they were magnificent-looking animals. The antlers of the bulls reached high and branched wide. Their brown bodies were marked cleanly by their great white-bearded chests. White bands circled their legs just above the hooves.

This was the time of harem-gathering and bitter fighting. The bunches that dotted the flat grazing area clear to the horizon were small groups of short-antlered cows, accompanied by their weaned calves and a few yearlings. A full-grown bull ruled each of these bands, guarding his cows jealously from rivals and seeking to bring the lone strays into his group. These lords of the herd rushed about day and night, eating nothing and losing the layers of fat built up through a summer of feeding. The cows grazed steadily and complacently. The younger bulls drifted along the edge of the broken herd, occasionally challenging an older bull, more often merely attempting to join the cows.

At the edge of a sinkhole, a great even depression in the flatlands caused by the melting and re-freezing of the earth above the permafrost level, a very old bull guarded the largest of the harems. Fully five feet high he stood at the shoulder. More than seven hundred pounds he weighed. His antlers branched like twin trees and his neck was swollen from battling with other bulls. The sharp polished tines of his antlers had pierced the hides of his rivals many times through the last month, the approach to the rutting season. Now his mastery was undisputed. A menacing shake of his rack, a sudden stomp of his hoof, and all other bulls would walk wide of his cows.

His giant, heavy-muscled shape and the long white vest beneath his massive antlers made him appear to be in the prime of life. Actually, like many of the powerful aged bulls, he was very nearly sterile. He was collecting cows now far more through habit and instinct than any interest in them. He guarded them vigorously. Yet his attempts at mating would be brief and halfhearted. When the seasons circled to the following May or June, the birthing time, his cows would be without calves.

Younger bulls, the ones that could produce those calves, watched his harem hopefully, even slipped up to try to nudge a cow aside and herd her away. But the old giant was far too watchful and cautious for them. Each time he charged they trotted quickly away. They knew he could not catch and punish them, for aged bulls can run even less rapidly than young calves. But they dared not attempt to stand before the menace of his horns and the weight behind them.

If bulls who had outgrown their fertility were allowed complete rule of a caribou herd, the species would disappear quickly. On the other hand, if each cow were to give birth to a healthy calf each year of her mature life, the herd would multiply far beyond the limits of the food supply and die of starvation. For once lichens have been overgrazed, at least twenty years is required to replenish these slow-growing plants. Somewhere between these extremes is a balance provided by natural wisdom.

And Nature has means of enforcing it.

Suddenly, a quarter-mile away, a group of caribou milled about uncertainly, then stampeded across the tundra. They ran with a high-stepping trot and their black noses were held so high that their faces were horizontal. Their gait looked awkward but the ground flowed swiftly beneath their hooves. Another bunch

38

of caribou joined the stampeding line, then another. The group at the edge of the sinkhole moved back and forth nervously. The old bull stamped his feet and shook his antlers once more.

A pair of timber wolves ran hard at the heels of the stampeding herd. They came over the flatlands at a steady and even lope, a pace that would not tire them through mile after mile of the chase. The male was slightly larger than his mate but neither of them weighed over a hundred pounds. They looked nothing like the creatures of human folklore—slathering demons, bright-eyed and with dripping jaws, slaughtering recklessly, murdering for sport. They were merely wild dogs, hunting for themselves instead of men, hunting as a means of life.

Feeding on caribou is hard work for wolves. A two-weeks-old calf can outrun the fastest wolf. This pair of wild hunters had been testing band after band throughout the early hours, driving at that same tireless lope, hoping to find a diseased or crippled animal. They had been unsucessful. Hunger still burned in their stomachs.

In February, just before whelping time, this wolf-pair had joined with many others to form a large pack. Often, just at dusk, they had surrounded bands of caribou and then begun howling, moving in with darkness. The pack had always been able to pull down caribou, but it had always suffered casualties. Any predator that lives by hunting creatures many times its own weight lives close to death. A wolf must move in close at a full run, dodge and slash, finally grip and pull the large animals to the earth while swinging by his teeth. If he goes down beneath the hooves of stampeding caribou he seldom rises again.

Just before the pups were due, the pack had broken up. Each wolf-couple had kept strictly to itself, turning punishing teeth on any invader of its denning site. There would be no more large packs until late the following winter. The hunting that was dangerous work for a team of thirty or more wolves was far more so for a single mated pair. But they were not hunting strictly for themselves now. In a dense thicket, a few miles back on the barrens, seven five-months-old pups had been left to sleep and wait.

The scattered bands of the caribou herd were now fusing into a single stampeding line. Several of the older bulls were dropping slightly behind, but none was running slowly enough for the wolves to single him out for attack. So they came on at the same pace, still testing and waiting.

The band at the edge of the sinkhole stirred restlessly for a few seconds. The cows and calves began racing wildly about, then broke into a trot and joined the stampede. The great bull tried to hold them back at first. Then, after pawing the ground and testing the air in the direction from which the scent of danger came, he too joined the race.

But the massive chest and head had grown far beyond the strength in his legs. The muscles that enabled him to defeat other caribou in combat were not the muscles meant for escaping wolves. The stampeding line moved on and he dropped slowly behind, even though he forced himself to his fullest trot; a labored lumbering gait with his face held to the sky.

The mated pair of wolves saw this at once, decided at once that the time had come to attempt a kill. The lope at which they had moved across miles of tundra suddenly gave way to a full driving run. Foot by foot they gained on the giant bull. And for each foot of gain a hundred yards of ground went beneath their racing feet, as the chase went over mile after mile of the level earth. When they finally drew abreast of the bull, forcing him to lower his head and slow down to fight, the line of the running herd was already small in the distance. Somewhere, far away, the caribou would calm down and begin to graze once more. And younger bulls would move quickly in rounding up the cows this old lord of the tundra had guarded.

When he lowered his head, the male wolf slashed in past his hind legs, trying from the beginning to hamstring him. The female dashed in front of him, ran sideways and even backwards just a few feet from his head, trying to keep his attention and provoke his attack.

40

The bull's first feeling, as he slowed his run and dipped his antlers to fight, was one of annoyance. He shook his horns and kicked out with his hooves much in the same manner he might twitch when mosquitoes became troublesome. For years he had run from wolves whenever the herd was attacked, but he had never felt their fangs himself. He had been stampeding from habit rather than fear. And he was not too much afraid now as he turned to give battle. He had ruled his herd for a long, long time. And these creatures were less than half his height.

He shook his antlers, then dropped them and bore down on the female wolf. She was facing him, but still moving away. The giant bull lunged, expecting to feel the weight of her body as the tines of his horns knifed through her. But he was lunging at a ghost-like shadow that sidestepped and leaped away. Instead, he felt fangs ripping deep into his hind legs.

The first cold waves of panic came over him then. He swung his antlers about but the male wolf held on like a bulldog, the terrible vise-grip of his jaws crushing and tearing. The bull kicked out with both hind legs and bucked like a wild stallion. One of his hooves caught the wolf a glancing blow on the shoulder. His jaws came loose. He cartwheeled in the air, landed on his side. He tried to rise and fell back. The wind was knocked out of him.

The caribou turned in deadly anger and raked hard with his horns. A tine of his right antler ripped along the wolf's neck, but once again he felt teeth sink into a hind leg. The female wolf was at his haunches now.

The bull bucked and kicked again. He felt his hooves land, felt bones break beneath them, but still the female wolf held on. The bull twisted and thrashed about frantically. He realized that he had only to rid himself of this sharp-fanged weight that swung from his leg and the fight would be his. He could turn and drive his antlers like nails into the fallen male wolf. Once he had shaken the female free she would not rise to threaten him again. He was certain of that. He had felt his hooves land many times.

But, dying as her jaws locked, the female wolf held on. Her mate was back on his feet now. Blood was running freely from his neck and his breath was coming in great labored gasps. He stood still a second, steadying himself. Then, with a bounding leap, he charged up to help the female, slashing madly at the other side of the bull's haunches.

The wolf severed the caribou's second tendon quickly and easily, biting through with his shear-like teeth.

Desperation and fear surged inside the aged bull when he could not shake loose the female wolf and turn to fight the male. He bucked high into the air in terror, twisting and kicking. Both rear hooves caught the female and ripped her free, sent her sprawling to lie still on the ground. But her jaws were still locked. When her teeth gave way the tendon of the bull's right rear leg gave way too.

He was hamstrung now.

His leg collapsed under him and he fell. Just as he was nearly to his feet again, the male wolf got the grip he sought on the other hind leg. The giant caribou bull could no longer buck or kick. The male wolf severed the left hind tendon quickly and easily, biting through with his shear-like back teeth.

The bull rolled on his side, his great flanks heaving and his hindquarters drenched with blood. Shuddering, he lay with his eyes open and waited for death.

But the surviving wolf did not strike again. He circled the fallen caribou once, then trotted over to where his mate lay. He sniffed her side, whining softly. He pawed several times at the fur of her neck. When there was no response he turned and trotted off.

The giant bull lay helpless on the ground, watching and wondering, as the figure of the wolf disappeared in the distance.

About five miles away the wolf climbed a slight rise through a thicket of short, stunted growth. In the first dim light of the false dawn he had stood with his mate on top of this rise and seen the long broken herd of caribou grazing on the flats. That had been several hours ago. Now he was badly bruised. His lungs ached and the jagged wound on his neck still bled. But the worst pain was a bitter loneliness. He felt the loss of his mate in a way that was very similar to human sorrow. His tail hung low and there was no spring in his step.

The pups rose from their hiding places and dashed to meet him, jumping up on his back, wagging their tails furiously. He nipped them, slashed lightly at them to quiet them. Then he turned and trotted back down the slope, moving slowly. The pups hurried after him. Their gait was awkward, but they were serious and orderly now.

Among the big cats, the puma and the jaguar, the male invariably kills the young if he finds them unprotected. The male bears do the same, leaving all responsibility for the cubs with the female. But a timber wolf family actually lives at a social level that is probably the equal of the life lived by primitive man. The male wolf that trotted back toward the hamstrung caribou had no thought but to continue caring for the pups, hunting their food for them and teaching them the lessons of staying alive. He would remain with them for two or even three years. Then he might possibly mate again. If not, he would merely wander across the vast tundra alone, hunting strictly for himself, snarling and unapproachable when he met other wolves.

A wolverine was stalking the helpless caribou bull.

The defeated giant had lain alone for hours. Several times he had tried to rise, but the throbbing pain in his hindquarters had always forced him to lie still again. For the last few minutes, sick with fear, he had watched the wolverine approach.

The newcomer was a short, stocky animal no larger than a cocker spaniel, with oversize teeth and claws. He had stalked carefully, long enough to learn the bull was helpless. Now he waded straight in for the kill, moving quickly in spite of his squat, bow-legged gait. His small flat eyes were greedy and eager.

He heard a soft whining sound and whipped around to face the intruder. The sound had been made by the male wolf. It was a signal that ordered the string of pups to scatter and lie flat in the sparse cover. They obeyed at once.

It is legend among the Eskimos and even northwoods whites that a full-grown timber wolf will give up a kill and turn and run from a wolverine. But no one has ever seen this take place and the male wolf had never heard the legend. He let out a low growl and began circling sideways. He was very tired and every muscle and joint in his body ached. But he had worked hard for this kill and his mate had died for it. No other wild hunter was going to steal it from him.

The wolverine advanced like a pit-terrier. The timber wolf kept on circling, silent now. Then, with a low hollow snarl, a blasting sound something like the scraping of wood on concrete, the wolverine rushed him.

The wolf dodged aside and slashed, leaped in and slashed again. His fangs opened a great flap of hide below the wolverine's ear. He was between the invader and the caribou bull now. He stood still and waited.

The wolverine screamed and snarled horribly in rage and pain. He made several quick, short advances toward the waiting

44

wolf. But he was merely bluffing now. Finally he turned and waddled off. On a slight rise, a few hundred yards away, he turned and looked back, sitting up and shielding his eyes with one paw. Then he lay down to wait.

Another low, soft sound came from the male wolf. The seven pups burst up suddenly from the short growth like rabbits being flushed. They scampered after their father.

All at once, the crippled bull caribou realized why the male wolf had not ripped the life from his throat hours ago. And the fear inside him tightened and twisted, a living and biting thing within him.

The male wolf had brought the whelps back to teach them to kill. The giant caribou bull was destined to be tortured to death by puppy teeth.

Like many functions of the wild, this was a cruel thing. Like all functions of the wild, it was a necessity. Caribou hunting is the only means of life the barrens wolves know. Caribou hunting is also a dangerous, involved occupation that must be learned from puppyhood. The first lesson the whelps were receiving was the same first lesson most human hunters give their dogs. A blooded hound is a pup that has been allowed to kill game deliberately crippled by the hunter's gun.

The torture lasted three hours. Caribou screams of pain are only grunts and finally even these ceased. Puppy teeth are sharp but puppy jaws are weak. The bull's hide was thoroughly chewed up, but none of the slashes was deep. At last the male wolf stepped up and ripped open the stomach cavity. The pups swarmed in and began gorging themselves, looking very much like a suckling brood on a giant grotesque female, shapeless and reddened.

The light in the air was failing when the wolf family trotted away from the kill, heavy and slow-moving with overfeeding, and started for the far-off security of thicket clumps that lay on their hunting runway.

The wolverine left his hiding place and swaggered down toward the carcass. He was a carrion-eater, but he was a hunter, too, a far different kind of hunter than the wolf. A bad-tempered animal who loved loneliness, he associated with others of his kind only for a few months when mating in February. The rest of his life he lived alone. He courted a different female each season and had no knowledge of his young.

But there was a strange fierce pride in his solitary existence. When the long winter came to the tundra, when constant blizzards and furious gales began smashing down from the Arctic Circle, the caribou would move south and the wolves would follow the caribou. The bears would hibernate. He would do neither. He alone, of all wild hunters, would stay in this land and depend on his predatory skill to carry him through.

He disappeared entirely into the stomach cavity of the bull. The light went out of the air. Night came over the barrens to hide the cruel and bitter yet vital and necessary end Nature had ordained for the once-magnificent lord of the caribou herd.

IV

THE WILD DOG—FABLES AND FACTS

THE wolf is merely a wild dog, with many generations of forest life behind him. Like the spaniel that dozes on your sofa or the boxer that guards your doorstep, his ancestry over the vast reach of more than seven thousand years has been a blending of wild and domestic strains.

The Early Neolithic men tamed dogs before they invented bows and arrows, before they planted grain. And the dogs they tamed were wolf dogs. Savage companions of savages, they were used for the hunt and the battle. Perhaps five thousand years ago they were taught to herd cattle. It is no accident that, except for coloring, the wolf is a near-perfect duplicate of today's collie and shepherd dog. The wolf was a domestic animal with the American Indians, who had no other dogs before those of Europe were introduced. From the writings of James Rosier in 1605 to the journals of the famed Audubon, this observation is made.

Today's wolf is an impressive creature. The remnant of the multitudes that prowled all the distances of pioneer America is a muscular giant, beautifully coated, an untiring and patient hunter of extreme intelligence. Somehow he seems to symbolize the untouched land of our continent, the virgin forests and clean rivers.

And yet popular belief paints a very strange picture of this animal that is really nothing more than a wild dog . . . a shark-like, ghost-like creature who will readily eat his mate and his brothers, but who prefers human flesh to all others and who sometimes drinks only the blood of his victims. Fantastically enough, it is even believed that this creature sometimes fills his stomach with mud. Above all, it is universally known that wolf pups can never be tamed.

Popular belief does not originate in wolf country. Cases of cannibalism among wolves are practically as rare as among men. The actual examples of wolves hunting and killing men that have occurred in the history of this continent may be numbered on the fingers of one hand. The wolf has no taste for mud. From our north-central states, across the entire breadth of Canada and all through the Alaskan wild, tame wolves live as dogs and breed with dogs, exactly as they have for seventy centuries.

This creature that popular belief supposes the wolf to be was fathered by an even more fantastic monster—a black, flame-eyed nightmare who lives only when the moon is full, hunts only humans, fears only the Christian cross and dies only with a wooden stake or a silver bullet through his heart. Most terrible of all, loup-garou is not an animal, the werewolf is really a man!

What naturalists can classify the creatures peculiar to the human mind? Who can tell where a superstition began? A minute incident with its momentary fear sometimes has a way of swelling beyond reason, then plunging ahead and breaking through time by its own momentum, snowballing across the centuries into something monstrous, a horror not of this world. Perhaps a Cro-Magnon chieftain was bitten by a wolf and went mad with hydrophobia and his tribesmen dropped back as his facial contortions began. So in our enlightened day a movie shows a group of travelers being followed by wolves, the leader howling as a signal to the leader of another pack to cut off the group. A TV story has wolves entering the streets of a large European city at night to hunt down human stragglers. And an intelligent, city-bred girl strolling past a zoo's wolf cage gasps in terror when one of the big gray captives glances her way.

Since a vastly remote age man has held two universal fears, intense and unreasonable, dwarfing all others—a fear of snakes and a fear of wolves. And these two images have dominated

48

mythology, folklore and legend, even religion. Christianity itself holds no symbol of wolf-fear, but it has never erased the older terrors—the Fenrus Wolf of the Eddas, the werewolf beliefs of both Europe and Asia, the Egyptian beast-god of Lycopolis, and all the other shadows that lurk in our minds, the shadows that are usually labeled black lycanthropy, from the Greek *lykanthropos*—literally, "wolf-man."

Strangely enough, side by side through the centuries, an opposite set of beliefs has existed—the legends that make up white lycanthropy, the tales of wolf-mothers raising children as members of a pack.

SCIENCE AT LAST ADMITS THAT WILD ANIMALS DO ADOPT BABIES! screamed the headlines of several American newspapers in 1939.

For five years the diary record of the Wolf-girls of Midnapore had been in the hands of a group of this nation's leading child-development experts and psychologists. They had examined it, checked it in every possible manner, asked every conceivable question. Now they were ready to state publicly that the story that follows was the truth:

On September 24, 1920, the Reverend J. A. L. Singh arrived at the little jungle village of Godamuri, about seventy miles from Calcutta. With a party of friends and native bearers, he had been ranging widely from his mission at Midnapore, seeking out the inhabitants of that uncharted wilderness. He found Godamuri in a state of panic. A *manush-bagha*, a man-ghost, was living in the jungle nearby.

The story interested Singh and he asked to be shown the spot where the man-ghost had last appeared. The natives gave him directions but refused to guide him. Their terror seemed somehow deeper than their usual superstitious fancies. Singh was certain that something real and alive had frightened them.

He followed their directions and found a giant, two-story ant-hill hidden in a gloomy jungle glade perhaps seven miles from the village. This, he'd been told, was the dwelling of the

49

man-ghost. He ordered his bearers to build a *machan*, a tree-platform used for tiger-shooting. Then he made a trip out of the bush to the nearest bit of civilization and obtained a pair of field glasses. He got back to Godamuri on October 8 and found his *machan* ready. With two Anglo-Indian friends, Richards and Rose, he took up the night watch in the jungle. The light faded from the air. The moon rose. They gripped their rifles tightly, watched the great white ant-hill and waited.

Suddenly they caught a glimpse of movement in the shadows of one of the caves. Something glided silently into the clearing. And there in the moonlight they recognized it. A wolf!

Singh lowered his rifle, puzzled. Was this the answer? Had an entire village been thrown into a state of hysteria merely because a few of the natives had seen a wolf? It seemed impossible. Another wolf followed the first.

Then all doubt was driven from his mind and he stared at the clearing in shocked horror.

Two creatures came from the ant-hill and entered the patches of moonlight, creatures such as a man could know only in the fantasy of nightmares.

The eyes of the wolf had gleamed yellow in moonlight. The eyes of these creatures gleamed a bright, piercing blue. They moved rapidly and easily on all fours, but there was no fur on their bodies. The heads could not be seen clearly under great masses of matted hair. One of them was much smaller than the other.

Richards gasped and lifted his rifle to his shoulder. But the Reverend Singh broke suddenly from the shock that held him, shoved the rifle aside and shouted.

"No! They're children! They're human children!"

At the sound of his voice all four of the creatures in the clearing below wheeled about and disappeared into the ant-hill again. Singh finally convinced his friends that he'd been right and they waited the rest of the night. But there was no further movement in the clearing below.

The next day Singh asked the help of the Godamuri natives in digging out the ant-hill. They refused, still terrified.

"You will leave, go far away," he was told. "We must live in this place. What will the *manush-bagha* do to us when his dwelling has been destroyed?"

All attempts to reason with them failed. Singh was finally forced to journey to another village and recruit a work-party there. He told them he wanted an ant-hill in the jungle dug up. He was careful not to tell them why. On October 17, the excavating began. At the first sounds of digging two wolves burst out of the ant-hill and escaped into the jungle.

Then the mother wolf made her stand. Snarling, her teeth bared in anger, she defended her home. With arrows and spears the natives made short work of her. In her last twisting, jerking convulsions, she looked like a giant pin-cushion.

The digging went on steadily. All at once, one whole side of the structure collapsed. The natives waited for the dust to clear. Then they dropped their tools and backed away in fear.

Two wolf-cubs and the two strange creatures that had once been human children huddled together in the corner of the den. All of them gave out high-pitched whines of fear and showed their teeth to the invaders.

For a few seconds Singh just stared at them. Legends of feral children have existed since before the days of Romulus and Remus, since even before the beginning of written history. But no one, even a missionary in one of the wildest sections of India, ever expects to meet such a monstrous rarity face to face. Now they could be seen clearly in daylight. There could be no doubt that they were human children.

Capturing them was a difficult, involved task. Cubs and children alike were giving vicious warning of what would happen to the hand of the first man that touched them. Singh finally got a large piece of cloth over them, separated them and tied them firmly. He gave the wolf cubs as presents to the natives who had helped him and started for Godamuri with the children. They were both girls. After studying them carefully he esti-

51

mated the age of the large one to be about eight years. The smaller, he was certain, was no older than a year and a half.

Singh stayed in Godamuri for some time and tamed the wolf-girls until they would accept the milk he brought them, lapping it from open bowls like dogs. Then he left them in the care of a villager and continued the expedition he had originally planned.

A week later he returned to Godamuri and found the entire village deserted. The natives had abandoned the children and fled in fear. Both of the wolf-girls were nearly dead from hunger and thirst, lying unconscious in their own filth. Great open sores had appeared on their skin. Furious with himself for leaving them, the missionary nursed them night and day, making a wick of a twisted rag and forcing them to suck milk, cleaning and bandaging them. After five days of constant care he bedded them down in an ox cart and began the long trip to Midnapore.

When he arrived on November 4 he told no one but his wife that the girls were feral children. Singh was in the habit of bringing back waifs from the jungle and the two new arrivals were accepted in the missionary's orphanage as abandoned children, nothing more. Mrs. Singh began the task of treating the large sores on their bodies. Within a month, their skin was clear and smooth once more, except for great calluses on their knees and elbows. With the massive tangles of matted hair trimmed from their heads, they looked almost human. But life among the wolves had left visible marks on them, even changes in body-structure.

Their arms and hands were abnormally long. Their big toes extended far beyond the others and turned upward on the ends, doubtlessly a result of running on all fours. Their jawbones seemed enlarged, almost double-jointed. Four of their front teeth had grown out of proportion, shockingly canine in appearance, and the color of the inside of their mouths was bright blood-red.

They could not walk or stand. They went about slowly on hands and knees. When they rose on all fours to run, they moved so rapidly that it was difficult for a grown man to catch them. In daytime, their eyes were mere slits. They seemed to fear the light. But in darkness, their eyes opened wide and large, a sort of blue light emitted from them, and they could see like cats. They drank milk readily but they preferred raw meat. Reverend Singh was afraid to let them have it because it brought back all of their original viciousness.

At regular intervals each night they howled—a strange and unearthly cry that was probably the nearest a young human throat could come to the call of a wolf. At approximately ten, again at one and again at three, this sound that was neither animal nor human would be heard. Several times the missionary took a lantern and went out to check on them when the cries came. He found them fast asleep, howling in their dreams.

More than once, the girls escaped from the orphanage and were found feeding on dead animals they had uncovered in the brush. One time the older girl drove vultures away from a dead chicken, snarling and biting at them, then ran off to hide and eat alone.

The older girl was named Kamala; the baby, Amala. They were at the Midnapore mission for six weeks before they would even move about, keeping to themselves all this time in the darkest corner they could find. But on December 21, Singh felt new hope for their eventual recovery. They made friends with a little boy at the orphanage, a waif who had himself been found abandoned in the jungle.

Ten days later, for no apparent reason, they turned on the boy, biting and scratching him severely. He never went near them again.

They never laughed and they never cried. They seemed never to be cold and never to be warm. In the middle of winter they refused to wear clothes, tearing them from their bodies as an animal might fight a trap. In the hottest days of summer no perspiration appeared on their skin. Instead, they panted. A warm day did not make them thirsty. They drank no more water during hot spells than they did in the coldest part of winter.

On January 29, 1921, they made their last attempt to escape, snarling and showing their teeth to the children who tried to stop them. A few days later their temperament changed abruptly and they came to Mrs. Singh to beg food. Amala, the baby, made the first attempt at speech. She said something that sounded like "bhoo, bhoo," when she wanted water. Next she learned to call Mrs. Singh "Ma." She had spent far less time in the wolf-den than Kamala, who had most likely lived as a wolf seven-and-a-half years. Perhaps it was only natural for the baby to learn the ways of humans faster.

Reverend Singh was certain Amala had been rescued young enough to make a quick recovery and then lead the life of a normal child. But on September 6, 1921, both girls suddenly became sick. For five days they were unconscious with bad fevers. Then attacks of diarrhea and dysentery came. Kamala slowly recovered, but on September 21, little Amala died. It was then that tears came to Kamala's eyes for the first time. But she was without expression. Her face muscles had not yet learned to show grief.

Amala's death was a serious setback to Kamala on her road to recovery. For a time she threatened to revert entirely to her previous animal level. She stayed in a corner for a week, refusing to eat or drink. After that she spent her time with the baby goats or the mission's pet hyena cub, but she shunned all human company. Sometimes she went about the orphanage on all fours for hours at a time, sniffing in various places where Amala had been and making a soft whining noise.

But finally there were a few scattered signs that the human in Kamala was winning its battle with the beast. By the end of November she was once again showing affection for Mrs. Singh. Shortly afterward she learned to nod her head to say yes.

Seven-and-a-half years in a wolf den had damaged her body as much as her mind. Each morning Mrs. Singh massaged her for a long period of time, attempted to loosen the deformed muscles that they might move in human fashion. A series of exercises was set up to teach her to stand and walk and she was kindly but firmly forced to go through them each day.

Rehabilitation was painful and slow for Kamala. She had learned to bring food up to her mouth rather than lower her mouth to the food, but she still lapped liquids. She still ate carrion whenever she could find it and would not touch salted meats.

In September of 1923 she was accidently locked out of the orphanage one night. Instead of running off into the jungle, she clawed at the door and howled to get back in. Later, she showed other signs of being afraid of the dark. The wolf in her was growing dim. By the end of 1924 she had a vocabulary of six words and could combine them.

The following year she learned to stand on two feet without help. She learned to like the taste of salt. She could distinguish colors.

By 1926 she was walking and her vocabulary included thirty words. She enjoyed her bath now and would not leave her room unless completely dressed. When one of the other children had a severe fall, Kamala ran to Mrs. Singh for help.

The next year her vocabulary increased to 45 words and she learned to sing simple songs. She was a far different creature now than the thing that had fought her captors in the wolf-den near Godamuri. She collected the eggs each morning for Mrs. Singh. She took care of the baby orphans. She laughed or cried, smiled or pouted. She had suddenly become afraid of dogs. At fifteen, she had reached the approximate level of a three-and-a-half-year-old normal child.

A certain group of scientists in the United States was becoming increasingly interested in Kamala. In 1928 the Psychological Society of New York pleaded with Singh to bring her to America. This was a difficult decision for the missionary to make. He carefully weighed the benefit she would receive from modern medicine against the harm publicity could do her. The question was decided for him. The girl suddenly became sick again and steadily grew worse. All thought of a trip was abandoned.

The frail little body had shouldered an immense burden in attempting to change from a wolf to a human. There was little strength left to battle disease. On November 14, 1929, with two doctors fighting to save her, Kamala died.

So the story of the wolf-girls ends, a strange little particle of Oriental mystery, a fascinating example of the enigma that is India. But ten years later, when the wolf-girl diary was unleashed in this country, it had become far more than a mere tale. Such men as Professor Zingg of Denver University and Professor Arnold Gesell, Director of the Yale University Clinic of Child Development, did entire books on the subject, not only accepting the story, but giving impregnable arguments for its authenticity and attacking any possibility of doubt. Professor Gates of the University of London, Professor Maxfield of Ohio State, and Professor Davis of Penn State all wrote prefaces to the diary when it was published. District Judge E. Waight of Midnapore and Bishop H. Pakenham-Walsh of Calcutta gave written statements of their certainty that the wolf-girl story was unembellished truth.

The men of science did not accept the diary-record idly or hurriedly. Five full years were spent in examining it, checking it against past tales of feral children, questioning Reverend Singh and in getting the opinions of their colleagues. They made themselves hard to convince, but the case seemed iron-clad. The missionary's diary was entirely consistent with other cases of feral children. The diary was accompanied by twenty-two Kodak snapshots, showing the wolf-girls in various poses. A long series of questions had been put to Singh and his answers had been satisfactory. The word of a judge and a bishop gave the story weight that could hardly be ignored.

So the tale was widely published, widely circulated and very few men raised questioning voices.

56

In spite of all this, the case of the wolf-girls of Midnapore was, beyond any possible doubt, a hoax. It is generally regarded as such today. The diary record was obviously faked.

The learned gentlemen who staked their reputations on the wolf-children story were undeniably experts in their fields. They knew all about child psychology and all about child development. They knew how to do research and present an extremely convincing analysis.

But not one of them knew anything about wolves.

If, during the five years they examined Singh's diary, they had allowed any naturalist a five-minute glance at it, they would have learned five very shocking facts.

First, wolves do not howl at regular intervals each night. This is folklore, but nonsense. Wolves have several distinct and separate cries, each with a different significance. There is no regularity to the use of any of them. By endowing the children with characteristics of legends about wolves, rather than wolves themselves, the diary-record loses all credibility.

Second, wolves do not perspire solely through their tongues. A good amount of their sweating is done through their feet and some is done through their skin. Besides, such a characteristic could never be acquired by association. Wolves feel temperature change every bit as much as we do. In the heat of summer they get very thirsty and drink a great deal of water. In the winter they sometimes freeze to death. Once again the children have been described as having wolf-traits that even wolves do not have.

Third, the milk of a mother wolf lasts only six to eight weeks, after which the young are fed a pure meat diet. It does not require an expert on child development to guess what would happen to a baby that attempted this transition. And wolf-parents force their own pups to hunt for themselves at two or three years of age. Kamala would never have been allowed to stay with the family seven-and-a-half years.

Fourth, the eyes of wolves or any other animals do not shine. They merely reflect light. Never does a "bright ray of light emit from them, illuminating objects" as the diary insists. There have been cases of reflective eyes occurring in human beings. But they are so fantastically rare that the chances of two children, both afflicted with this phenomenon, being brought together in any coincidental manner can be discounted. Besides, in every recorded case of reflective eyes among human beings, the color of the gleam was red or orange, never blue.

Fifth and most startling of all, there are no wolves in the jungle around Godamuri or Midnapore or anywhere else in the eastern half of India. Canis lupus has the widest range of any carnivorous animal in the world, but that range includes very little of India. Only in the hills of the northwest is he found. Even there the wolves are rare. When this bit of information was first brought to light, one of the scientists who had leaped on the wolf-girl bandwagon without looking, hurriedly insisted that if it wasn't *canis lupus* it must have been *canis pallipes*. In other words, if wolves didn't raise those girls, jackals must have. But the credibility of the tale had already been shattered.

Once a wedge has been driven into the wall of authenticity and respectability the men of science built around the story, other inconsistencies take on new meaning. Neither Richards nor Rose could ever be found to confirm the missionary's account of what happened at Godamuri. Evidently not too much effort went toward the task of locating them. All of the photographic evidence is blurred and inconclusive. There are no close-ups. Any of the pictures could have been easily posed by normal children.

The case of the wolf-girls of Midnapore remains a mystery. But the puzzle is not how a mother wolf managed to adopt, suckle and raise a human baby. Rather it is how an isolated missionary with no access to libraries or medical files and records managed to manufacture a case history that completely hoodwinked the experts of the world. In that respect the hoax is a classic and deserves to rank with that of the Piltdown Man.

As contradictory and ridiculous as lycanthropy of any color is, it can hardly be lightly dismissed. Wolf-fear is very, very real, today as through all time. Lycanthropy is more than superstition. It is an actual medical term, a classified form of insanity still prevalent as a disease throughout Southern Europe and Asia. And its origin poses one of history's most maddening and evasive puzzles.

Why are we so afraid of wolves?

There are theories. It is likely that before the advent of modern firearms wolves were far bolder than they are today, although even in country where they are never hunted, they rarely attack man. A professor of anthropology recently suggested to me that wild-dog packs, raiding villages, even cities, as packs of recently-gone-wild dogs do today, offer an explanation. I have even heard the theory that wolf-fear goes back over twenty-five thousand years to the prehistoric dire-wolf or cave-wolf, a creature no more closely related to today's wolf than a woolly mammoth is to an elephant.

And yet none of these suggestions is really satisfactory. Runaway dogs regain their respect and fear of men in the second and third wild generations. Their depredations are slight. And the dire-wolf skeletons that have been brought up from the California tar-pits indicate that the late Pleistocene wolf was smaller than today's timber wolf. It is true that giant wolves, monstrous wolves, once walked this earth. A few of their skulls have been found in China. But their time was long before the coming of true man.

The best explanation I can offer for wolf-fear and wolf-superstition is the possibility that rabies was once far more widespread and common than it is today, that it was in fact one of the great plagues of the early, unrecorded years.

One thing is certain—very certain. The wolf, as he exists today, is no mirroring of the wolf-like shadows in the backs of our own minds.

Still, even to the naturalist, the wolf seems an animal of mystery. Some wildlife texts refer to all the strains throughout North America as gray wolves. Others classify a dozen or more species. The best and most complete studies indicate that there are but two American wolves.

The coyote-like red wolf of the Southwest, *canis niger*, the rarer of the two, is an ancient native of this land. He has no brothers or even close cousins among Old World wolves.

The big timber wolf or gray wolf, *canis lupus*, is most likely an immigrant. He is the "true wolf" and his range is world-wide. Perhaps ten thousand years ago his migration from Asia began as he followed his food supply, sometimes hunting for himself, sometimes living as the servant and pet of the immigrants who became American Indians. There are twenty-three substrains of timber wolves on this continent today.

At the time the white man first came to this country, the range of the wolf included every bit of North America. Today, timber wolves are still fairly plentiful in certain sections of Alaska and Canada. But within the United States they are so scarce that a very slight reduction in numbers would mean their going the way of the passenger pigeon, the bison and the sea-otter. There are a few timber wolves left in the Cascade Mountains of Oregon and their number has remained constant for more than twenty years now. The big gray fellows occasionally come up from below the border to range through the wildest sections of Arizona and New Mexico. But the last refuge of the timber wolf in this country actually exists in the great northern forests of Michigan, Wisconsin and Minnesota.

Red wolves are still holding out in Oklahoma, Missouri, Texas, Arkansas and Louisiana.

Nearly all wolves in the United States today live on national forests. And this brings out an interesting point. The extermination of wolves throughout this country was brought about, not by the armies of private and government predator-control men with their poison and traplines and finally airplanes, not by the gigantic sums of money we've spent on bounties, but by civilization's destruction of suitable wolf-range and civilization's slaughter of the wolf's food supply.

Timber and red wolves are similar in habits, similar in nearly

60

everything except size. Red wolves average about thirty-five pounds, with perhaps seventy pounds being the upper limit. Timber wolves vary greatly in size, ranging from the weight of large red wolves up to such specimens as the one-hundred-and-seventy-five-pound wolf killed by Frank Glaser, a Fish and Wildlife Service predator-control man, on the Seventy-Mile River in Alaska in 1939. (Frank claims no record. He insists a two-hundred-and-twelve-pound wolf was killed the year before.)

Wolves of both breeds have five distinct and separate cries, each with a different significance. There is the soft, high-pitched whine the parents make to the pups. There is a guttural howl, loud and deep, usually followed by barking, and this is a hunting call. There is the cry of the chase, a sharp yelping sound something like the bawl and chop voices of foxhounds. There is the cry of the kill, a deep growl with a heavy blasting sound, a little like the snarl of the wolverine. But the famous call, the howl of lonely winter nights that has pierced human imagination most deeply and seems designed to freeze a human victim's blood with terror, is actually a mating cry. Wolves breed in mid-winter.

The thick, double-coated mats of wolf-hides are as varied in color as the wide-scattered stretches of wolf-country, for it is believed that these animals take their coloring from the amount of light, moisture and other conditions in the cover they prowl. The dominant color-phase is usually gray. Far more red wolves are gray than red. There is a certain tendency for the darker wolves to be more common in such places as the swamps of Louisiana and the light-colored wolves to be found more often in the Arctic, but this is by no means a hard and fast rule. Almost forty percent of the wolves killed recently in Alaska have been black or dark gray. Twenty percent of Alaskan wolves are predominantly white. A pure white wolf, however, is a thousand-in-one rarity. Brown wolves are common on the Alaskan range. The wolves of our north-central states are usually gray. In Ontario, they're often grayish-yellow.

The wolf is probably the most intelligent of all wild animals. This conclusion is inescapable if estimates of animal mentality are based upon observation in the field and study of habits and characteristics, rather than by the testing of caged specimens.

The center of life among wolves is the family. The legendary "pack," described in whole libraries of fiction as a disciplined organization with teamwork, tradition and an all-powerful leader, simply does not exist. At certain times, such as a moose or caribou migration, several families may combine to form groups of fifty or more animals, but these unions are always very short-lived.

Once family life among wolves is understood, it is impossible to comprehend where the concept of this creature as a cold-blooded, unfeeling, unthinking brute could have had its origin. A wolf family usually has its beginning in December, when a two-and-a-half year old female, who has left her parents a few months earlier to hunt for herself, comes into heat. Young males start leaving their families at this mid-winter time and the un-earthly mating calls begin sounding across the frozen forest night. Courtship lasts a month and a half, a percentage of life-span equivalent of a year and three months in human time. Several young males may battle for a certain female's favor, but she is as likely as not to choose the loser and stand beside him in facing other suitors. If there is a full moon, a mating moon, during the last weeks of courtship, the howling becomes a constant sound throughout wolf-country. The mating, once consummated, is for life.

The mated wolves cover great distances during late January and early February, running together each night and lying up in the brush during the day, wandering far from the hunting runways of their parents. But life is short and there is work to be done. The wolf-couple choose their hunting-ground, then set themselves to the two tasks of building dens and bringing in a meat supply.

The wolves prepare several dens for each whelping season. As many as four may be used for the same litter. They are never located too far from hunting runways and are usually on hill-sides. Sometimes they are caves in rock or limestone. They may be enlarged rabbit or badger holes or even caverns dug completely by the wolves themselves. Sometimes they are made in abandoned beaver dams. The new dens may be a few hundred yards apart. They may be several miles.

At the same time meat must be found in great quantity. The worst slaughter of deer, sheep, caribou, elk and moose begins in mid-February and lasts until the first of April. Very often far more game will be killed than can be eaten and only the tongues may be taken at first. This has caused a number of observers, coming across these kills, to describe the wolf as a creature that hunts for sport. The fact that the heavy slaughtering is only done just before the pups come indicates strongly that the wolves are merely preparing themselves for a time when they cannot leave the area of the dens to follow the migrating herds. If left unmolested by man, these kills are invariably cleaned up.

Contrary to the teachings of thousands of adventure stories the wolves that are crippled in the hunt are not turned upon and eaten by their mates and their brothers. Instead, they are helped in every way possible until they either recover or die. They are guarded constantly against the possibility of attack by grizzly or puma. Food is carried to them.

A female wolf may have her pups unexpectedly when some distance from her den. When this happens, she seeks out any convenient thicket for the birth, but the pups are carried one by one to the den shortly afterward.

There are usually five to eight pups in a litter, although there may be as many as fourteen. Their eyes open in about a week. They are most often gray-brown at birth. In regions where the white phase of the wolf is predominant, they may be a light blue or slate color. Their smooth coats become shaggier as their puppy teeth grow, developing steadily into their first winter coat. When they shed to their summer coat at about a year of age, they gain their adult color.

The floor of a wolf den is remarkably clean. The parents never foul the den with their leavings and they even carry the waste matter of the pups outside. However, most dens have a very strong smell that is unpleasant to the human nose. This is caused by the buried hoard of meat nearby and by the method of weaning the young—swallowing great quantities of flesh and returning it to the den and disgorging it in piles for the pups to eat. Sooner or later, the rotting meat smell and the flies and insects it attracts make the den location offensive even to wolf nostrils. Then the family moves on to the next den, previously prepared.

The pups are weaned when six to eight weeks old. By this time they have been venturing outside the den for a month or more. Their parents bring them food from a distance of as much as twenty miles, often carrying large bones for teeth-cutting, but at this time they hunt in a straight line to and from their home. The male wolf seldom enters the den. He usually spends the day at a good look-out point from which he can keep watch. He never sleeps soundly during whelping time. If human beings approach, he sends out a warning cry to his mate, then howls loudly to attract the attention of the invaders, often showing himself in an attempt to distract them from his home.

The last den is abandoned when the pups are about three months old. The family starts out on its hunting-runway, often a hundred-mile circle in country where game is scarce. No longer do the wolves bring food to the young. They make a kill and bring the young to the spot to feed. The pups remain at the kill, sleeping and playing while their parents hunt again.

In August and September, when the teeth of the pups are strong enough, the wolf-couple begins training them to hunt and to kill. When they are about eighteen months old the pups are large enough to hunt as a team with their parents, often routing game and driving it along in full cry while the older wolves wait in ambush to make the kill.

Female pups remain with their parents until they are slightly over two years old. Male pups mature a little more slowly and sometimes remain three full years. When new litters are born, the yearling pups from the last year's litter help the parents build up the meat supply, prepare the dens and guard the whelps.

The big cats and the bears may be lone prowlers, but the wolf is a family man.

V

THE WAR WITH THE WOLVES

SOMEDAY I hope to see a Hollywood producer attempt the making of a realistic Western movie—a picture that would tell the true story of the grim struggle the cattle-raising industry fought for existence, the life-or-death battle that raged for more than a half-century from Texas to Montana.

In such a movie no silk-shirted young man in polished boots would ride hard over the plains pursued by thousands of howling Apaches, mowing them down by the hundreds with blazing six-guns. No silent stranger would ride into some little town, free it from outlaw rule and then ride on into the sunset.

Instead, a line-rider would come across the butchered carcasses of a half-dozen calves in some remote corner of the winter range. And a government wolf-hunter with a string of traps in his pack would ride out through great distances of lonely country, following the big dog-like tracks in the snow.

The West wasn't won with a Colt pistol or a Winchester rifle. In the longest, costliest, most vital and vicious fight of all, the Number Four steel trap was the weapon. If the rewards offered for every badman in American history were added up, the total would be a mere fraction of the hundred million dollars this nation has spent on bounties. No human rustler could match his fame against that of the Sycan Wolf, the White Wolf of Cheyenne, the Pryor Creek Wolf or Lobo, the King of Currumpaw.

But the most notorious outlaw of all was a big male wolf that ranged the Black Hills of South Dakota, a four-footed rustler

66

who was known as the Custer Wolf. The cattlemen of that area claimed that this renegade had been raiding their herds for nine years and had caused well over $25,000 worth of damage. They pointed out that, with $500 on his head, dozens of the West's most skillful hunters had tried to get this wolf and failed. They insisted the Custer Wolf had powers that bordered on the supernatural, that he'd made slaves out of two coyotes and taught them to guard his flanks and warn him of danger whenever he crossed open range.

Strangely enough, all of these things were true.

Early in 1920, Dr. Nelson of the Biological Survey called in a young government hunter named H. P. Williams and spent many hours going over the thousands of complaints the Department of Agriculture had received from the area where the Custer Wolf raided. Then he shook Williams' hand and said,

"It's all up to you now."

A few days later Williams was riding into the Black Hills west of Pringle. He'd studied enough reports and talked to enough ranchers to learn that the Custer Wolf might be found anywhere in a rectangle about 40 by 65 miles. He'd also learned that the residents of the region firmly believed that nothing short of old age could ever kill the Custer Wolf. In fact the local cattlemen had made little attempt to hide their belief that the Biological Survey was sending a boy to do a job at which many men had failed.

Williams knew that all outlaw wolves have one main weakness. There is always a pattern of regularity in their habits. After mapping the most recent raids of this wolf, he was certain that the outlaw was lying up somewhere in the Pelgar Mountains. He scouted this country and found fresh tracks. But catching a glimpse of the Custer Wolf was a far more difficult task.

The hunter had been told that, four years before, the Custer Wolf's mate had been killed and that the old outlaw wolf was now the last remaining wolf in the region. It was said that he'd adopted and trained the two coyotes only after his mate was gone. In return for acting as his sentries they were allowed to clean up his kills when he'd eaten his fill.

Williams had never really believed the tales of the Custer Wolf's two coyote servants. But the tracks he found were convincing and incontrovertible. The smaller animals stayed between one and two hundred yards from the wolf, one on either side. After they'd ruined a half-dozen attempts Williams made at stalking, he was forced to shoot them both. But he was still unable to get the old outlaw in his rifle sights.

Next, he tried using female wolf-scent on his boots and setting out a number of traps. He managed to trick the wolf into believing a female was using his runway. The old renegade even dug a new den to prepare for the mating. But he still walked wide of the traps and of his pursuer.

For several weeks the Custer Wolf played a game of hide and seek with Williams. Several times the hunter discovered that the wolf had circled back on his trail, as if amusing himself by watching the efforts of the man. Then, late in April, the Custer Wolf suddenly disappeared.

Not until August was he heard from again, when he raided some cattle on the far side of his range. Williams patiently went to work in this new region, setting out his traps and making attempts at stalking once more. One day he was almost within rifle range when a cowboy rode up unexpectedly to spook the wolf.

On October 11, 1920, after seven months of constant work, Williams discovered that the Custer Wolf had stumbled into one of his traps but had managed to pull the chain-stake out of the ground and drag the entire set off. Williams tracked rapidly for three miles and finally shot the old outlaw.

The South Dakota telephone exchanges were tied up the entire night as the news spread. Most of the state's papers carried a simple headline the following morning: THE CUSTER WOLF IS DEAD! When Williams started back to report to Dr. Nelson, he took the skull and the white-haired hide with him.

The Custer Wolf was doubtlessly the most famous of the

68

West's animal outlaws. But the most stirring and dramatic story in all wolf-warfare came a couple of years later in the Butler's Pasture region of Colorado. This case-history was carefully investigated and preserved by Dr. Stanley P. Young, Senior Biologist of the U.S. Fish and Wildlife Service. There cannot be the slightest possible doubt of its authenticity.

A winter night had closed down on the range, blanketing the Apishapa River country with cold and stillness. The cowhands at the headquarters ranch of Monroe Brothers and Henerson were in bed when the sound came, a sound none of them had ever expected to hear again.

It was a prolonged wailing howl, deep and painful, as dismal a note as ever heard by human ear. It grew from those mournful tones, swelling up and up in the night until it became a thunderous scream, like the whistles and braked steel wheels of a dozen freight trains screeching toward disaster in darkness. Then, as it softened, its pitch became more piercing, it vibrated on the spines and nerve ends of the listeners, they felt it rather than heard it until it faded and died, holding all cold and loneliness in its last gasp and in the silence that followed.

No one who had ever before heard that cry, shimmering and strange in the night, could forget it. It was the mating call of a gray wolf.

The men at the ranch leaped from their bunks, pulled coats and boots on, snatched rifles from racks and hurried out. In the yard of the ranch house, their big male pedigree collie was barking steadily. He followed as they ran up a small knoll at the rear of the corral, the direction from which the wolf call had come.

Lanterns were lit on the hillside. But there was no movement in the brush. A circle of light finally picked up the tracks where they led off into the night. Several men knelt to examine them.

The print of the front left foot showed two missing toes.

"Her, all right!" a man muttered.

The collie stood erect and stared off across the vast open range, whining softly.

It was 1922 and the cattlemen of Colorado had just become certain that a long hard battle was finally being won. For many years they had fought the herd-raiding wolves just as their fathers before them had fought the Indians. They had lost far more cattle to the big gray killers than to rustlers.

But the herd-owners were breathing easier now.

Old Lefty of Burns Hole was dead. Lefty had been caught in a trap back in 1913 down in Eagle County, but he'd bitten his leg off to free himself. He'd kept on raiding the beef for eight more years, running on three legs, and he'd killed 384 head of livestock. Then he'd gotten another foot in a trap and he'd been unable to gnaw it free before the trapper made his rounds.

Rags the Digger had finally stepped into a blind-set trap. Rags was well known for his trick of digging up traps without springing them and for his extremely shaggy appearance. He raided the cattle in the Cathedral Bluffs area for fourteen years and did ten thousand dollars' worth of damage. There was no mistaking his track when he made a kill. His hind feet were longer than his front, just the reverse of the way most wolves are built.

The Unaweep Wolf, the Queen Wolf of Whitewater, was now stuffed and in a museum in Denver. She had led a raider pack a dozen strong, causing terrific losses to the herds. But she too had at last stepped into a blind set.

Big Foot, the Terror of the Lane Country, had been killed. This wolf made a track so huge it barely fitted inside a Number Two horseshoe. His raids were so frequent and destructive that the cattlemen were tying bells on their cattle in hopes of frightening him away. He was finally trapped, along with his three-legged mate, on a runway leading to his den.

The Phantom Wolf of Fruita was dead. The Greenhorn Wolf of the Butler's Pasture had been taken. One by one, the great outlaw lobos of Colorado had become victims of skillfully-placed

70

traplines. An era was passing. Never before in history had such intelligent wild creatures given battle to the advance of civilization. Never before had the abilities of human hunters and trappers been put to such a test. The renegade predators had become so wise in the way of man's efforts to destroy them that their uncanny powers were truly unnerving. They were able to scent the steel of traps and the poison of baits. They knew when a man was armed and when he was not, merely by sniffing his trail. Entire communities had hunted them. Gigantic hound packs had run their trails. And always, even from the men who were suffering most from their raids, they commanded respect. A human outlaw was a violator of the laws of men. But an outlaw wolf was living in full accord with the laws of Nature.

Bit by bit, civilization had won its battle. The wolves of that cattle-raising state had gone down the long trail to oblivion blazed by the bison, their former means of life. Only one remained now. Eagerly, and yet with a tinge of sadness, the stockmen waited for her death.

Three Toes, they called her—Old Three Toes, the Widow of the Apishapa.

Dawn came, cold and gray. A rider from the Monroe Brothers and Henerson spread started up the river to check the stock on a nearby section of winter range. His breath was white in the sharp air and his hands were clenched in the pockets of his windbreaker.

He had just worked his way carefully through the thickness of a swale, then given the horse the rein again when he saw the calf. Two turkey buzzards croaked in complaint as they winged their way clumsily up over the brink of a ridge and disappeared.

The rider dismounted and looked over the butchered calf. There was no mistaking the work of a wolf. A puma would have attacked the head or neck. A grizzly would have broken its back and dragged it off. Only a wolf would have attacked the flank and ripped through to disembowel its prey. On livestock, a wolf eats and kills at the same time, attacking, feeding and leaving in a matter of minutes. Very often the calf is still alive when the wolf leaves. Sometimes, if a wolf attacks a calf and eats his fill on a haunch, the calf recovers, marked of course by an enormous scar.

There were no tracks to be found in the brush. The rider climbed on up to the top of the ridge and searched along an open stretch of bare sandy earth. Only a short section of the trail where the killer had loped off was visible, but one identifying print was clear and distinct.

This was Three Toes' work, all right.

The rider mounted once more, turned and spurred back for the ranch.

No one understood the strange antics of Colorado's last wolf, even government trapper Roy Spangler, whose main assignment for some time now had been the task of putting an end to Three Toes' raids. Why had the wise old female wolf come to the ranch house and howled on a night she was making a kill? Was she mocking the men whose herds she raided? Was she merely sending a cry of loneliness up into the winter night, protesting the emptiness of the vast miles of range, the country where she would never again find the track of another of her kind?

Or was she actually looking for a mate?

Three Toes had not always been a lone wolf. A little more than a year before she'd been the mate of an unusually clever outlaw wolf the stockmen called Old Whitey, a pure white wolf so large that his track could barely be covered by the palm of a man's hand.

In the fifteen years that Whitey was known in the cattle country, every method known to the best of the trappers failed to get him. The ranchers were insisting set-guns be tried, the government hunters protesting this was too dangerous. Old Whitey settled the controversy and surprised everyone, including himself, by stepping into an ordinary blind-set trap in 1921.

Nothing further was seen of his equally famous mate, Three Toes, in the country around Bear Springs Mesa. The stockmen held their breath, hoping she'd died of old age and her carcass lay hidden in some unknown canyon, hoping Colorado was finally free of wolves. But the three-toed track suddenly appeared in the Apishapa River country, the area locally known as Butler's Pasture, where the Greenhorn Wolf had made his raids years before.

The old widow wolf was still feeding on cattle. Every four or five days through 1922 a butchered calf would be found, most of them on the Monroe Brothers and Henerson range. But the cattlemen and government trappers were still hopeful, even when the best of their efforts failed to get the wise old wolf. They were certain she was the last one left. Time was on their side. Three Toes couldn't live too much longer. And, without a mate, the raids would end with her death.

The wolf call split the night apart once more. The collie was barking with a strange, high-pitched urgency.

Then that evening in December came the forgotten sound of a wolf call. And everyone waited and wondered.

Three days after the slaughtered calf was found in the river range, there came a heavy-clouded afternoon, then an early nightfall. Darkness became pitch blackness without moon or stars. The men at the headquarters ranch hurried through the evening chores and sought their beds early.

They woke abruptly a little before midnight. The wolf call was splitting the night apart once more.

Cowhands and foremen alike leaped from their bunks, groped about to find clothing and lanterns and rifles, then hurried out into darkness. On the other side of the yard the collie was barking steadily. But he sounded nothing like a ranch dog threatening an invader. There was a strange, high-pitched urgency in his barking, not a warning or a challenge. It was more as though he were troubled by feelings he didn't understand.

Two of the ranch hands left the stream of men who were hurrying toward the knoll where that eerie cry was sounding again. They listened to the collie's barking a few seconds.

"He's answering her!" one of them gasped in disbelief.

They started across the yard. One more wolf call came from the cover above the knoll, much farther away now. Then silence surged back. The barking had ended, too.

They ran to the kennel. The collie was gone. They shouted his name as they hurried toward the knoll, stumbling and crashing their way through the growth. They joined the rest of the men, who were searching out the area with lanterns flashing and rifles held ready.

"Careful what you shoot at!" they yelled. "The dog's up here, too."

The warning was hardly needed. Nothing stirred in the cover. None of the searchers caught the slightest glimpse of movement. Like a gray ghost, the old widow wolf had vanished after her bold appearance on the ridge. There was no further sign of the collie, either.

A long search on a cloudy night would have been futile. The men made brief plans for a mounted party to start after the dog at dawn, then hurried back to their bunks.

But when they rose in the dim light of earliest morning, the collie was asleep in his kennel. He thumped his tail in a tired, half-hearted manner, then closed his eyes again.

74

Most cattlemen would have shot a ranch dog that ran off with a wolf. But the big collie was far more than a watch dog. He was the favorite and pet of everyone, a beautiful and high-bred animal. Moreover, he was worth a great deal of money.

There was an abandoned chicken runway on the ranch, a sturdy enclosure made of six feet of strong fencing with a base of one-by-twelve lumber. The collie was thoroughly scolded by his owners, then locked inside.

"You just sit there and look pretty," he was told. "Three Toes'll learn there's more than one kind of trap. You'll make real nice bait."

The dog began barking in protest the minute he was penned. When darkness came that night, he was still barking. And the men who stood watch with their rifles, hidden in the brush of the knoll, listened with satisfaction. He'd call the old female wolf right down to their gunsights.

But there was no sound or sight of Three Toes that night.

Perhaps the intelligence that enabled the wary old lobo to kill thousands of dollars' worth of sheep and cattle and remain alive to continue raiding allowed her to sense the trap and avoid it. Perhaps tame and wild dogs alike have understanding and sounds of communication more advanced than men have ever believed, and something in the collie's bark was a warning. At any rate Three Toes never came near the knoll. Night after night the hunters waited. But nothing moved in the thickness.

The stockmen relaxed their guard slightly, hoping the old female wolf was gone from their part of the state. But a night came when that mating call sounded in the winter air again, this time in the cover on the far side of the ranch. The collie barked eagerly. His owners hurried over with their rifles loaded. Once more they found nothing.

Again the next night and the night after that the wolf-howl and the collie's barking shattered the stillness. The bushy out-law vagabond paid her court and the fine thoroughbred yapped his acceptance. Something in the mating cry of the wolf drove everything from the collie's mind that five thousand years of domesticity and select breeding had instilled. It was as though he sensed something wild and sweet and compelling in that call, something more desirable than all the favors of civilization. The food that was placed in his pen was left untouched. Even in the daytime now he paced the wire fence nervously.

Three Toes wasn't undergoing any loss of appetite herself. Even in her ardor for finding a mate, she took the time to select a few of the choicest calves on the nearby winter range. And the efforts to destroy her became frenzied and desperate. Traps were set in every likely spot throughout the surrounding cover. Poison baits littered the area. Riflemen waited in ambush. But Three Toes' raids went on. And somehow, again and again, she managed to slip through the gauntlet and loudly declare her devotion to the caged collie.

Suddenly a night of silence came—no wolf cry and no barking. The cattlemen rose at dawn, eager to set out and ride their trap-lines, certain that the old female wolf had finally stepped into the wrong clump of brush. But they stopped short in the yard.

The pen was empty. A mound of fresh earth was heaped beside it and another dirtpile lay within the wire. Three Toes had come into the very shadow of the bunkhouse to dig the collie out. He'd followed her example and they'd worked together until the hole beneath the ground-board was large enough for him to slip through.

He was never seen alive again.

The measures used to get Three Toes became even more frantic. Poison baits were now spread not only in the cover surrounding the ranch, but also throughout the open range.

There is and has always been a bitter prejudice against the use of strychnine in any sort of predator-control work. But actually, if the history of wolf-warfare is examined, poison was one of the more kindly weapons of civilization. The wolf's method of killing his prey may be cruel at times. But the devices of men for exterminating wolves have always been far more so.

At one time, the use of fish-hooks was popular. In the years when wolves were less wary, it was a common practice for settlers to wire three large cod hooks together to form a treble hook, bait it with meat and hang it from the branch of a tree, four or five feet from the ground. Rising on his hind legs to get the meat, a wolf would be hooked in the mouth and held fast. Suspended and tortured for days, he'd either die of starvation or be killed when the trapper made his rounds.

But the wolves of Three Toes' day were far too clever for any such method.

In the north country, "piercers" were a favorite weapon against wolves. Thin, sharp lengths of whalebone were bent into the form of a spiral spring and cased in pieces of frozen seal fat. When a wolf swallowed this bait, the fat thawed and the bone pierced his stomach. This method worked for a time. But all baits failed when wolves learned it was unsafe to eat anything they had not themselves killed.

Variations of this method were used in New England. Baits were made by dipping pieces of broken glass in tallow until they were about the size of an egg. Thousands of these were scattered throughout the forest.

Deadfalls are illegal practically everywhere today, but they were common when wolves still ranged the greater part of this country. Nearly every pioneer farm had a wolf-pit, often with pointed stakes at the bottom to impale the trapped animal. And if all else failed to exterminate wolves, the early settlers thought nothing of setting the forest afire.

Set-guns were not too ancient a wolf-killing device. They'd even been considered for use against Old Whitey, Three Toes' former mate. A shotgun or rifle was tied to a stump or boulder. A cord was fastened to the trigger, then run through a screw-eye on the butt of the stock and back to a bait placed on the muzzle. Set-guns killed far more humans and cattle than wolves.

Strychnine poisoning became widespread in the days of the professional wolfers, the fur-hunters who roamed the plains killing buffalo and poisoning the carcasses, then merely picking up the wolves and coyotes and foxes who came to feed. But the use of strychnine carried over to the years when cattle came to the flatlands. At one time it was more or less of an unwritten law in Colorado that any cowboy finding the body of a steer would poison it in the hope of killing just one more wolf.

Few men have ever attempted to hunt down a wolf. Organized hunting, even with large groups of men and dogs, has usually failed. Ben Lilly was the greatest of the predator-hunters and yet he never attempted tracking wolves. Only one man, government hunter Bill Cozzens of Idaho, was really successful in stalking the big lobos. Bill would start out on skis, completely dressed in white, after each fresh snowfall. He was a skillful enough skier, a rapid enough tracker and an accurate enough rifleman to kill wolves in this manner.

For most government hunters, the steel trap was the stock weapon. When men like Spangler were assigned to a certain wolf, they studied the record of its kills and analyzed its droppings like an engineer doing research for a scientific project. They mapped its runways carefully, listed each of its mannerisms and peculiarities. They sought always the wolf's weakest point—the regularity of its habits.

These professional predator-killers were skilled and capable. It might take them a good deal of time to end the depredations of the particular wolf they hunted, but chances were the cattlemen and the private bounty hunters had been after that wolf for years and failed.

Each government predator-trapper had secret methods, individual techniques he never revealed. But these men seemed to have one thing in common. Almost without exception, they were opposed to the use of poison.

At the time Three Toes lured the collie off, Spangler had been arguing steadily that scattering strychnine baits throughout the range was doing no good, in fact was interfering with his work by keeping the old female wolf on guard. But with the collie's disappearance, the poisoning program was merely stepped up. It took a more dramatic lesson to show the futility of this method.

Three weeks after the thoroughbred ranch dog ran away his body was found near one of the poison stations. The tracks plainly showed that Three Toes had been with him at the time he'd eaten the strychnine-loaded bait. But the wolf had tested none of the poison herself.

The strychnine baits were taken up. Spangler went on about his work, using in general the same system that finished off the greatest of the outlaw wolves.

After painstakingly determining the runways Three Toes used, he went over them to find what were known as scent posts. These were bushes or clumps of grass where wolves habitually stopped, wet the ground and scratched before continuing along the trail. By sniffing these posts a wolf could determine many things about the others of its kind that had passed—their identity, their sex, even whether or not they had recently fed.

Once the scent posts on Three Toes' runways were located, Spangler prepared his traps. To kill any odor that had been accumulated, he boiled them in water and hemlock bark. He then dug holes the size of the traps near the scent posts, kneeling on a square of rawhide as he worked and placing all of the dirt carefully on the hide. The traps were set in these holes, bedded firmly and anchored with a six-foot chain and a stake-pin. A pyramid of dirt was built up over the trap and around the edges of the pan. A small cover made of canvas or screen rested on this wall of earth and hid the pan. A half-inch of dried dirt covered the entire set. The surplus earth was carried off in the hide and scattered at a distance.

Three Toes was the last wolf left on the runway so it was necessary to make the scent posts attractive. Most government hunters obtained natural scent from the carcasses of wolves they had previously killed. They took the urine, the gall and the anal glands, added an ounce of glycerine to every three ounces of the mixture to prevent evaporation and a grain of corrosive sublimate to prevent spoiling. Sometimes an artificial scent was made from decaying fish, but this smell was also attractive to cattle and could not be used on the open range.

The wolf scent was placed on the posts along the runway and renewed every four or five days, more often if the weather was wet. The gloves and shoes of the trapper had to be scented also.

To get a wolf as wary as Three Toes, every scent post on her runway had to be trapped and revisited regularly. Since wolf runways were often more than a hundred miles in length, the task facing Spangler was an enormous one.

For many months he went about his work and rode his lines without encouragement. There was no evidence that Three Toes had been using her runway. In fact, there was no sign of her anywhere along the Apishapa. She'd vanished from this stretch of range just as completely as she had from the Bear Springs Mesa area after Old Whitey's death. But the government trapper kept the scent posts of her runway freshly sprinkled. If she ever returned it might be possible to convince her that a male wolf was using her runway. Once she began showing interest in the scent posts, it would only be a matter of time until she stepped into a set.

The loneliness and yearning of the call Three Toes had sent up into the December night was being taken fully into account. Her need for a mate would be the weakness made to work against her.

The Colorado spring dried itself to summer. Three Toes had been very nearly forgotten along the Apishapa when the night of June 8 came and the hands at the Monroe Brothers and Henerson ranch sensed the increasing restlessness of the herd on the summer range. Riders set out in darkness to calm the stock, but not until dawn was the cause discovered.

Six young calves lay butchered in the moist grass.

The three-toed track was found near the site of the kill, but it was obvious from the amount of flesh torn from the carcasses that the raid was the work of a pack. The search went on until a section of the out-trail was found where the ground was soft and the tracks distinct. A careful study revealed that five pups were now running with the old female wolf.

Near-panic spread among the cattlemen. Poison baits might have littered the countryside once more. Dangerous set-guns might have been rigged in the brush along the river, now that Three Toes was back on her runway. But the careful preparations Spangler had made paid off.

On June 11, 1923, Three Toes, the Widow of the Apishapa, the last wolf in Colorado, stepped into one of his traps.

Recognition seldom came to the government trappers. In one rare instance, the man who killed a wolf in South Dakota, after it had been hunted in vain by 150 men over a thirteen-year period and killed fifty thousand dollars' worth of livestock, was awarded a gold watch by the ranch-owners. But, except for a brief thank-you note from Monroe Brothers and Henerson to the Fish and Wildlife Service, Spangler's feat went unheralded.

He went on about the task of trapping coyotes and also decided to attempt capturing the wolf-collie whelps. That same June he roped two of them from horseback. In August he roped another and his trapline accounted for the remaining two.

Four of the crossbreeds were dark-colored and favored their mother in appearance and temperament. Taming them was impossible and they were put to death. The fifth, a female, looked very much like a collie except that her red hair was tipped with gray and her muzzle and ears were those of a wolf. She was kept alive and turned over to Dr. E. J. Foreman, a veterinarian in Trinidad, Colorado, for breeding.

The wolf-dog was first coupled with an Airedale. The pups of this litter were tame enough, but nervous and suspicious. One of these males was later bred to a German Shepherd female. The resulting whelps were all extremely gentle and affectionate. Only a few traces remained of their wild inheritance. They preferred to sleep outside, even in cold weather. Their trot resembled a wolf's pace.

So the blood of Colorado's last cattle-killing wolf was passed on to pets and fireside companions of men, dogs who lived their lives knowing nothing of the deeds of their famous outlaw ancestor.

The record of the gray wolf in the West was the story of his long struggle with the livestock industry for supremacy. And the success or failure of cattle-raising in the United States depended very much on the outcome. It seems somehow ironically justified that the former buffalo wolves turned to killing livestock, since their previous food supply had been exterminated by men. Today, the war with the wolves is history in this country. The big gray predators are very nearly extinct and, with a few exceptions, the men who fought them are dead.

Recently, on Lake Superior's Isle Royal, an attempt was made to restock the dwindling wolf population by setting zoo-raised animals free. This didn't work. Instead of answering the call of the wild, the wolves stayed close to the resort end of the island, feeding out of garbage cans and attempting to romp with the tourists.

Things have changed a great deal since the time, little more than thirty years ago, when Three Toes ruled the Apishapa, selecting the choicest calves for her meals and slipping through whole armies of armed hunters, mine-fields of strychnine and steel traps, to find a mate.

VI

WOLVES THAT HUNT MEN

BACK in Michigan's lumbering days, a camp boss named O. S. Whitmore set out from the headquarters of a cutting near the Upper Manistee River to check on a scaler's cabin about three-quarters of a mile to the north. It was late afternoon of the day before Christmas and the shadows of the trees were lengthening.

Whitmore found the cabin deserted. The crew at that lonely wilderness outpost had left their work early to join the other jacks for whatever celebrations were possible in the Michigan northwoods. The lumber boss stayed some time at the cabin, making a systematic inspection. He found a Christmas package of stale baked goods and threw them out.

A few minutes later, he heard a snuffling sound in the snow beyond the log wall. His first thought was of a large dog owned by the cook in the main camp. He decided to call the dog inside. This was timber wolf country. The winter had been unusually severe and the wild things were starving. Every night the jacks had heard the chase cries of the big gray brutes as they ran down deer in the deep snow.

Whitmore opened the cabin door. In the failing light, he caught a glimpse of a large animal dodging back into the brush. He called out several times, but no dog appeared. Closing the door, he finished up his work, lit a lantern and started back for the main camp.

Whitmore was too seasoned a veteran of the northwoods to consider himself in any danger from the marauding wolf packs.

He'd seen wolves in the forest many times in his life. At the sight of a man they invariably tucked their tails between their legs and disappeared like ghosts. The lumber boss had heard and read of man-hunting wolves. But, like most men who really know the northern forests, he laughed at such stories.

Just the same, he picked up a small hatchet from the cabin wood box and carried it with him.

Darkness had come suddenly. Beyond the circle of lantern light, Whitmore could see nothing. He felt the bitter cold as he went down the trail and he hurried briskly along.

All at once, he stood still. He was certain he'd heard the sound of other crunching steps in the snow, but nothing disturbed the forest stillness now. Laughing at his own uneasiness, he started on.

Suddenly he stopped again. Now he was certain of it. Something was moving up the trail behind him. Once more, the noises cut out. He held the lantern high, but he could see nothing.

He kept moving on toward camp, fighting an impulse to run. The soft sounds of padded feet on snow came from both sides of him now and the steps behind him were drawing closer. He turned quickly and whirled the lantern around. This time he caught the gleam of several pairs of eyes before his pursuers dodged back into cover.

The impossible was happening. He was being hunted by wolves.

Trying desperately to keep his nerve, Whitmore turned and kept walking. He could just barely see the dim, faraway lights of the camp that meant safety. Every ten yards or so, he turned and swung his lantern at the creatures behind him. The big gray beasts were getting bolder. They stood their ground until he lunged at them with the lantern. Then they dodged back once more. But when Whitmore started on he could hear them patiently following.

The lumber boss was less than a quarter-mile from the camp now and he felt confident he could make it. The wolves seemed to be very much afraid of the lantern. He turned and swung it at them once more.

The bottom came loose and fell to the snow. The flame held on for a few seconds and then died.

Terrified now, Whitmore shifted the hatchet to his right hand and backed away slowly. The rush came almost immediately. In the faint, cold starlight he could just barely make out a giant form leaping toward him.

He swung the hatchet with all his strength and felt it smash into bone, but the weight of the wolf knocked him sprawling in the snow and the hatchet flew out of his hand. He scrambled to his feet and ran, screaming insanely. He crashed into a tree, fell again, then grabbed a branch and started climbing.

Only one other wolf was bold enough to attack. The powerful, sharp-fanged jaws caught the heel of Whitmore's boot and held on, dragging him back. He kicked out with the other foot. The heel came free and he pulled himself up higher, still shouting at the top of his lungs. Wolves were swarming about the base of the tree now. Yelping cries of impatience and hunger were sounding in their throats.

Then the slam of a cabin door echoed across the snow. Voices rang out. And the entire crew of big husky jacks came racing down the trail, armed with rifles and clubs and knives, spoiling for action. Six wolves were killed before the others gave up and ran.

Whitmore studied the attack scene very carefully later. There was no doubt that the wolves were in an extreme state of starvation. The metal of the broken lantern was covered with teeth marks and the whale oil had been gulped from the snow.

The timber or gray wolf has been man's most feared and hated enemy as far back as history is written. Throughout all recorded time, a bitter war of extermination has been waged against him. Today, that war is very nearly over. In all but a few sections of his former range, the wolf is either extinct or on the brink of extinction. With typically human inconsistency, it has become the present-day fashion for naturalists to insist that wolves have never preyed on men.

Some years back, a Canadian hunting guide named John A. Hope became involved in a lengthy discussion of this age-old question, a question that has been debated as often in zoological circles as in the smoky warmth of little northwoods taverns:

Is or is not the timber wolf a man-hunter?

John Hope had lived his entire life in wolf country. He had never heard of a wolf attacking a man and he considered all stories of killer wolves to be pure fiction. He argued the case for the negative, argued it quite heatedly, in fact.

A few days later he stumbled onto a unique opportunity for an unusual experiment.

He was making the rounds of his trapline when he heard wolves running a deer in the nearby forest. In the cover beside a large lake, he stood still and listened to the chase. The snow was not too deep. The deer had a fair chance of winning the grim contest.

The wolves were singing for blood now. Their sharp, ringing chase cries came closer and closer.

Suddenly a young buck broke cover a half-mile down the shoreline and went straight out across the ice at a full run. Less than a hundred yards behind came a half-dozen wolves. The buck stumbled and slid about on the frozen lake but he managed to keep his lead until he disappeared into the timber of the far shore.

Somehow, the buck outran or outwitted the hungry pack. About fifteen minutes later John Hope saw the tired wolves trot out from the other shore and lie down to rest on the ice, about a thousand yards away.

As John Hope watched them, he thought of his recent argument. Suddenly he realized that this was a perfect chance to prove his point conclusively.

He stepped out from cover onto the open ice, waved his arms to attract the wolves' attention and then stood still, expecting to see them bolt for the brush. Instantly, all six of the big gray fellows jumped to their feet and ran. But they ran the wrong way—directly toward him!

John Hope stared at them, unbelieving. On and on, the pack came, racing down upon him with startling swiftness. When they were about two hundred yards off they broke their tight formation and spread out in a fan-shaped line to encircle him.

Hope snapped out of the shock that held him, flipped his rifle to his shoulder and threw two quick shots that exploded the ice in front of the charging pack. An abrupt change came over the gray beasts. They dug in, skidded as they turned, then fled for the nearest bit of cover.

John Hope always insisted afterward that these wolves must have mistaken him for the deer they'd just lost and couldn't really have intended to attack a man. But he never made a test like that again.

In the ever-recurring debate on the question John Hope was attempting to settle, both sides have made some ridiculous claims. Fictitious stories of man-hunting wolves have never been scarce. On the other hand, a good many articles have recently been written that claimed to prove no one was ever slain or even attacked by a wolf. This "proof" usually consists of merely repeating one well-known fact and overlooking many others.

For over 35 years now, the U. S. Fish and Wildlife Service has investigated every rumor of wolves killing men that came to its attention. Not one such report has been accepted by the authorities.

Actually, this fact proves only two things: first, that the timber wolf has been very nearly exterminated; second, that modern flat-trajectory cartridges have instilled a deep fear of man in the handful of wolves that are left. In most recent cases where wolves have attempted to hunt men, the mere sound of a rifle shot has been enough to send them running.

In the winter of 1937, a Canadian trapper named Ralph Edwards was making the rounds of his line near the coast range of British Columbia, walking directly down the center of the frozen Atnarko River toward Lonesome Lake, armed only with a single-shot .22 rifle. He had a blizzard in his face and he could see almost nothing. Some trick cleared the air for a second and he caught a glimpse of seven gray forms coming directly toward him. He dropped his pack, loaded the little rifle and waited.

The wolves spread out to surround him, one large brindled animal moving well ahead of the others. Edwards decided to try and make a break for the cover of the shoreline, but a black wolf dashed around and cut him off. The trapper stood still and the wolves kept moving in.

When the big brindled wolf was about fifty yards off, Edwards lifted his rifle. His first cartridge failed and the wolf kept on coming. The trapper frantically ejected the shell, shoved in another and fired. At the sound of the shot, the entire pack turned and ran.

The next spring Edwards was attacked by four wolves. He was walking through tight cover, studying the trail in front of him, when some premonition made him look behind him. The wolves were less than ten yards away, already spreading out for the attack. Luckily, the trapper was carrying an automatic rifle of heavy caliber at the time. After five rapid shots at point-blank range, two of the wolves lay dead and the others were heading back into the hills at full speed.

Another argument made by naturalists who refuse to classify the timber wolf as a possible predator of man is that the wolf is basically a wild dog. And this is true. The ancestry of the wolf has always been a mingling of wild and domestic strains. Even today, some habits and characteristics of the timber wolf make it seem likely that a certain subconscious and instinctive memory of domesticity still remains.

But any claim that this aspect of wolf-nature will prevent the big gray fellows from attacking man overlooks the fact that wild dogs themselves often join together in packs and become a serious menace to human life. The Adirondack Mountains of New York have long been the hunting grounds of such creatures. Hounds and collies, boxers and Danes alike have answered the call of the wild, learned to hunt for themselves and made a

88

number of unprovoked attacks on human beings. As a matter of fact, dogs that have recently gone wild are far more dangerous than wolves. They have no reason to fear man, no reason to turn and run at the sound of a rifle shot.

Once the report of a wolf attack appears in the newspapers, the task of tracking the story down and learning the truth is very likely to be tedious and unrewarding. But such cases can also be humorous.

Some time ago the Toronto *Globe* published a story of an old trapper being torn to pieces and eaten by wolves on a wilderness trail about 70 miles north of Ignace. Immediately, a flood of letters came from residents of that country. They had never heard of such an attack. One of them, obviously a bachelor, was especially vehement.

"We been trying to get women to move into these parts," he wrote. "Do you think stories like that are going to help things any?"

Not far away, in Sault Ste. Marie, Ontario, editor Curran of the *Star* once offered a large reward for proof of a wolf attack. This offer was kept open and publicized for many years, but there were no takers. Just as this editor was giving up and writing a book entitled *Wolves Don't Bite*, a claim was made for the reward. It came from a doctor in Pennsylvania. He asserted that a wolf he keeps caged up in his backyard bit one of his guests. Curran didn't pay off on this claim, but it did provide an interesting new chapter for his book when it was published.

Reports of wolf attacks still drift down from Alaska quite frequently. Here in the States they've become extremely rare. The Iron Mountain wolf scare was probably the most recent.

It all began with a fairly short column in the Iron Mountain *News* on November 8, 1954, under the heading, WOMAN TELLS OF BATTLE BETWEEN WOLF AND DEER. It opened, "Is the daddy of all timber wolves roaming the forest in the Merrimen district of Dickinson County?" It told, simply and plainly, that a housewife near Merrimen had seen a large wolf chasing a buck on her farm. One other citizen of Merrimen, the story went on, had also seen a large wolf recently. Nothing more.

Then the story arrived in the newspapers of the downstate Michigan cities. The headline had now become BIG TIMBER WOLF SCARES U.P. FOLKS. The lead had changed even more: "A huge gray timber wolf, brazenly stalking livestock and even human beings, is causing frightened residents north of Iron Mountain to stick close to their homes these days." The story went on to mention the wolf-deer chase, then claimed a resident of Iron Mountain had seen the wolf stalking a woman near Merrimen, two other people had seen the wolf, the local men were guarding their children as they waited for the school buses, an organized hunt was being planned and conservation officers were warning deer hunters.

I was in New York at the time and this was the form in which the story first came to my attention. I remembered, as I read it, that a Michigan black bear had killed and eaten a small child farther east in the Upper Peninsula six years earlier. It was remotely possible that one of Michigan's few remaining wolves had turned outlaw. Hunting down a man-hunting wolf would be a once-in-a-lifetime experience. If an organized hunt was being planned I wanted to be in on it and I hurriedly wrote Dr. Whitlock of Game Research at the Michigan Department of Conservation headquarters at Lansing.

But before I received an answer the story broke in the big New York newspapers.

REIGN OF TERROR! the headline screamed. Now children were being closely guarded throughout the entire Upper Peninsula. The farmers didn't dare venture from their homes unless heavily armed. Livestock was disappearing at an alarming rate. Several people had been stalked by the terrifying monster. It was just a matter of time before he got someone.

The day after the big-circulation New York dailies finished with this example of professional journalism, I received a letter from Ivan Thompson, the District Game Supervisor at Crystal Falls, Michigan.

90

"I would like to state that there seems to be some exaggeration somewhere along the line on the wolf story that was released in Iron Mountain on November 8. As far as we can find out, no one here seems to know anything of this wolf having stalked any human beings. Neither was there any effort by anyone in the neighborhood to hunt down the wolf. The story did not cause too much concern among local people when it broke in the paper. However, there were a large number of downstate deer hunters in the area within the next few days. It did cause some concern among them."

Mr. Thompson then went on to describe a visit to the lady who had first seen the wolf.

"I asked her if she had ever seen wolves before. She stated she had not. I asked her if she didn't think it might have been a dog. The identification might be right or wrong. I don't know how we could say."

The very great majority of tales about killer wolves are manufactured in exactly this same manner. It's quite understandable that, after tracking down a few dozen such reports and finding them false, a naturalist might come to the conclusion that all such stories are fiction.

Actually, however, there can be little doubt that timber wolves have, on extremely rare occasions, made unprovoked attacks on human beings.

There is no animal on this continent better equipped for hunting and killing a man than a timber wolf. No other creature is his equal when it comes to intelligence, hunting ability, stealth in stalking and suddenness of attack. Both the size and fighting ability of the gray wolf are seldom realized. Alone, he is usually more than a match for any other creature in the forest with the possible exception of the grizzly. Nothing in the wild can stand before a wolf pack.

The gray ghosts of the North most certainly have the ability to successfully hunt man. Possibly, a remembrance of domesticity plays a part in holding them back. More likely, their fear of man and his weapons is the main factor. But, since man did not always have those weapons, wolves did not always have that fear. And even today, hunger can become stronger than fear.

The wolf has had the reputation of being a man-killer for many, many centuries. When incidents become legends, they are of course exaggerated fantastically. But there is usually a hard kernel of truth beneath them. Old World history is filled with accounts of wolf attacks. In several European countries, the ruins of structures designed to give travelers protection against wolf-packs are still visible. If one percent of the wolf stories that have come out of Russia are true, the Siberian packs are definitely a menace at times. In the last few years a steady stream of wolf-killings has been reported in northwest India.

In America, attacks by wolves have always been very rare. But pioneer journals from every part of this country make some mention of raiding wolves.

The Wolf Hills section of Abingdon, Virginia, got its name from an attack made on the famed frontiersman Daniel Boone. A hungry wolf pack raided his camp one night in the Valley of the Holston. Boone and his companions drove the fierce creatures off only after a long and furious battle.

A regional history of Pennsylvania mentions a Dr. Thorton who became lost while attempting to find the wilderness cabin of a patient. Thorton was surrounded and attacked by a band of wolves. A two-day skirmish followed. The doctor saved himself by pouring a bottle of ammonia on one of his leggings and striking at the big gray killers with it whenever they got too close.

Most wolf attacks have always been the result of starvation. But a wolf inflicted with rabies, especially the violent form, was a universal frontier terror. Mad wolves appeared most frequently in the early spring. They were always alone. Exactly like a rabid dog, they kept moving constantly and slashed at everything that came into reach.

If an Indian brave was bitten by a mad wolf, the medicine men of his tribe immediately had him bound with raw buffalo hide, then hung over a bonfire. If he survived, he was pronounced cured. The early white men were no more humane. The records of the fur trade show that the Mountain Men usually abandoned any of the party unfortunate enough to contract rabies. Very seldom did they waste precious powder and lead putting a comrade out of his misery.

There have been a few wolf attacks in which the animal involved was neither starving nor rabid. Almost a century ago, an eighteen-year-old girl started out to bring in the cows on a farm beside the Little Snake River in Moffat County, Colorado. Sitting perfectly still on the slope above the path, she spotted a large gray wolf. Instead of running off, it merely watched her. She shouted at the top of her lungs. The wolf let out a low warning snarl. She picked up a rock and threw it. Instantly, the wolf came bounding down, leaped on her and threw her to the ground. Her screams brought her brother, who shot the animal in time to save her life, but her legs and arms were badly torn. The wolf was a young one, well-fed and definitely not rabid. The conclusion that he'd jumped the girl out of pure meanness seemed inescapable.

Very few of the attacks made in this country have resulted in death. Throughout the entire reach of American history, only four fatalities have been recorded.

The reliable and respected naturalist, John Audubon, claimed to have personal knowledge of a wolf-killing that took place in Kentucky in the early 1820's. Two young Negro men who lived near the Ohio River were in the habit of crossing a four-mile-wide stretch of cane-brake every night to see girls on another plantation. Bears, lions and wolves were still plentiful in that area and the two men carried axes with them. They were surrounded and attacked by several wolves and a desperate battle followed. When one man went down under the weight of the beasts, the other managed to pull himself up a tree. Badly wounded, he stayed there the entire night. In the light of dawn he found three wolf carcasses. The bones of his friend were scattered over the entire area.

During an expedition to the Far North, an early naturalist-

93

explorer, John Richardson, investigated and accepted as true a case of a wolf attacking and killing an Eskimo woman.

A more definite and incontrovertible account comes from a later Arctic explorer, Donald B. MacMillan. A half-breed Eskimo who had accompanied MacMillan was ripped to pieces and eaten by wolves.

The most recent incident that seems to qualify as a wolf-killing took place in 1933 in Alaska. A sixty-year-old trapper named John Millovich left Fairbanks in the spring and started for his cabin, 75 miles to the north. He was expected back in a few weeks. When he failed to return by mid-summer, two friends decided to check up on him.

They found what was left of him in the cabin yard. Every bit of flesh had been torn from his bones. The entire area was covered with wolf tracks. It seemed obvious that the old trapper had started for a nearby water hole without his rifle and had been surrounded, killed and eaten by wolves.

Some years later, when a detailed investigation was made, it was decided that this case could not be accepted as scientific proof of a wolf attack. Since no one had actually witnessed the incident, it was remotely possible that the trapper had dropped dead of a stroke or a heart attack and that wolves had merely fed on the corpse at a later time.

Most Alaskan old-timers shook their heads at this decision of the authorities and pointed out that wolves are very, very reluctant to feed on carrion. It seems only sensible to consider Millovich's death a wolf-killing. A good many human beings have gone to the gallows, the electric chair or the gas chamber on less evidence than existed here.

Four fatalities in more than three centuries is not very many. There have been far more cases of cannibalism, of man-eating men, in American history than cases of man-eating wolves. By no stretch of the imagination do the few times the big gray fellows have been the aggressors justify the extermination of this species or the unbelievable amounts we've spent on bounties.

Today, the timber wolf is disappearing rapidly. In spite of

94

this, stories of man-hunting wolves will continue to appear. The very great majority of them, in the future as in the past, will be either mistaken or deliberately false. Because of this, many naturalists will continue to assert that all killer wolves are and have always been products of human imagination.

But all too often the men who classify the habits and characteristics of wild animals overlook their extreme variation in character. It is true that normal wild wolves do not attack human beings. But abnormal wolves, whether starving or rabid or just plain mean, can hardly be identified at a distance. Hiking alone and without a rifle through country where wolves are still plentiful, especially in the months when the families have combined into larger packs, is simply not an intelligent thing to do.

You might have a stroke or a heart attack.

VII

THE TRAIL TO EXTINCTION

WOLF-HUNTING, as a sport, has few devotees. All wolf country is lonely country. Wolf tracks lead on forever in the roughest of terrain. Only by the use of airplanes and buckshot does a hunter have any real expectation of success. And most outdoorsmen have different ideas of recreation.

But, even though chases are successful perhaps once in twenty times, the running of wolves with dogs is a compelling sport. It breeds fanatics. Once you have crouched near a clearing, excitement driving the cold from your body and your hands tingling on your rifle, once you have listened to a big hound's voice tearing the air apart and waited for a wolf to break cover, you cannot easily go back to jumping rabbits from brushpiles or flushing pheasants from cornfields. And even the hounding of foxes and bobcats may seem tame.

The breeds of dogs that earned the name of wolfhound for themselves in Europe and Asia are rarely used on American wolves. Old World wolfhounds were primarily gaze-hounds, sight-running hunters with little scenting ability, and are useless in the thickness of this country's forests. The borzoi or White Russian Wolfhound may be a marvel on the flat barren steppes. In America, he's nothing more than a stylish city-dweller's pet. The gigantic Irish Wolfhound was always more of a livestock guard than a hunter.

In the southwest red wolves have been run with oversize Walker and Trigg foxhounds that are blooded on wolves and bred especially for this type of chase. Wolfhound trials have been held, much like the foxhunts of the East. The hounds are faster, the game far more elusive. For in spite of the fox's legendary reputation for skill ahead of hunters, the wolf holds the thicker country, knows far more cover and often turns on his trail to change a foxhound's mind about becoming a wolf-hound.

The timber wolf is larger, more ferocious and a prowler of more impenetrable cover. The fast, hot-nosed dogs of the Southern foxhound clan are of little use on his trail, since he can either leave them behind in the drifted snows of the northern forests or turn at bay to tear up an entire pack of them in a manner that would ridicule the occasional stories of his cowardice outdoor writers produce. Long-eared, cold-nosed dogs work best here, the breeds that make no attempt to catch and fight their game but merely drive it ahead to a waiting hunter's rifle, hounds whose bugling voices are mighty enough to keep an elephant fearful and moving. As always, when heavy game is hounded in the north country, the old native blueticks and black and tans are the favorites.

Most wolf-killing is extermination, not hunting. The government predator-control men and professional wolfers who killed off the wolves of our West used traplines, poison baits and finally airplanes. Very few men have ever attempted to match their own skill and intelligence against that of the wolf.

Even in timber-wolf country, where the need for predator control is slight, extermination methods are still used. Airplanes, strychnine and cyanide are the stock weapons of the Alaskan wolfers. In Canada and our north central states hounds and hunters alike sometimes cruise the islet-strewn shores of the larger lakes in fast, propellor-driven sleds, searching out wolf tracks. An island is found with a wolf-line leading in and no tracks leading out. And the element of chance or of sport is completely erased. Hounds flush the wolf from the cover. Hunters run him down on the ice in the aero-sleigh.

Extermination methods are more than ways of killing wolves. They are part of the deeply rooted fear of these animals that seems to govern our state legislatures, some of our outdoor writers and our federal wildlife program. Since bounties first came to the colonies in 1630, most American wolves have been hunted outlaws who live with a price on their heads. Nowhere are they protected at any time of year in this country.

There is no quicker plan for uselessly depleting a state's fish and game fund than through a bounty system. All of our sportsmen's magazines have repeated this opinion editorially again and again. Few hunters have any desire to see their license fees used to destroy any form of wildlife. Experts have proven with monotonous regularity just how fantastically little predator control has to do with the size of the deer herd, the pheasant crop or the rabbit cycles. And yet year after year state legislatures, harassed by pressure groups of the minority who wish to convert our forests to pasture and suffer from the modern-day remnants of lycanthropy, block the attempts of sportsmen to remove the bounties.

Both of our American wolves face absolute extermination today. There is a precarious level below which extinction will be almost immediate. The wolves' numbers remain tightly at that level in all but a few sections of their range.

The wolf's survival is really a much more serious question than the fate of one species. The wolf symbolizes our untouched land, but he does more than that. In a very real sense, he guards our wilderness. *Always, when the last wolf is killed off, a stretch of good country, clean and green, is on its way to becoming pasture or farmland. Always.*

The great forests of Michigan, Wisconsin and Minnesota are usually considered the last refuge of the timber wolf in the United States. And yet a recent study has revealed that the permanent wolf population of Michigan's Upper Peninsula consists of only twelve wolves—that is, six pairs are alive to reproduce each winter, the yearly bounty crop being anywhere between twenty-five and thirty. The situation in Wisconsin and Minnesota is very much the same.

In Alaska and in the Canadian Yukon a gigantic government

program is underway to destroy the wolf. The U. S. Fish and Wildlife Service is carrying on this extermination supposedly to protect the caribou. But it is doubtful that any wildlife authority really believes the wolves are responsible for what has happened to the caribou herds. The caribou have been reduced more by men in the last three hundred years than by wolves throughout all history.

Some of the very same men who exterminated the wolf in Washington and Montana are active in predator-control work in Alaska today. Their memories are short, for they repeatedly insist the Alaskan wolf could never be driven into extinction.

For a startling preview of Alaska's future I wish I could take some of the men who believe so strongly in predator control for a drive up through Gaylord, through the heart of Michigan's forest-lake country, to the wild land that lines the Pigeon River. There are elk here, in forest that looks as untouched as Hiawatha country, but is actually second-growth. For this was once lumbering land. And when the pine went, the native elk herd went, too, and finally the wolves.

The pine has come back. A few decades are but a moment in time. The elk have come back, too, shipped over from the Jackson Hole country in Wyoming by a conservation commission with a dream of creating a great new game animal for Michigan's modern hunting army. But you can read the printed snow of this forest again and again through a winter. There are no wolf tracks.

There is also no elk hunting. Six years after the stocking, Department Director John Baird predicted that in the very near future there would be a short open season. The herd size at that time was three hundred animals. The prediction did not come true. In cover that is ideal elk cover, *protected and free from all predators,* the herd suddenly refused to prosper, and today, after twenty-eight years, still numbers only a few hundred animals.

A number of theories have been offered as to why this herd failed to multiply. The best and most obvious reason was well stated recently by Otto Failing, Game Division head of the Gaylord District, in an article in *Michigan Conservation*.

"The birth rate is at a fraction of its proper level. We believe the shooting of a few large bulls each year would improve the health and vitality of the herd."

Mr. Failing continued the thought in correspondence with me.

"I believe more emphasis should be placed on the laws of nature. There is no doubt in my mind that predators are as necessary in the scheme of things as the game animal upon which they prey. It might interest you to know that in 1953 Michigan paid $152,985 for bounties and has been paying bounties on wolves since 1838. Not a pretty picture, is it?"

Each species, Darwin pointed out, *develops itself over centuries for survival under a given set of conditions. The removal or extreme altering of these conditions, even the seemingly helpful destruction of a predator species, upsets delicate natural balances, introduces factors for which the species is unprepared.* Now we must selectively kill off the older bull elk in the region north of Gaylord to compensate for the lack of wolves. Socialism, in our forests as in our national finances, is a one-way street with no end.

Let's face the truth. We're not "controlling" wolves in Alaska today. We're fighting with them over caribou meat. If we win, and we always do, the caribou will hardly benefit. Wolves have demonstrated throughout countless centuries that they can live off the interest and let the capital remain. This is something men have yet to prove they can do.

The fate of the caribou herds and the fate of the caribou-hunting wolves are permanently entwined and cannot be separated. This is not theory but a simple statement of a basic principle of biotic balances. Nature's own game-management program, remember, has been tested over great distances of time.

Also in Gaylord, you might meet a red-plaid-shirted, slightly alcoholic old-timer who will tell you very confidentially that he

100

himself killed the last wolf in Michigan's lower peninsula. At any northwoods bar in the stretch of forest and farmland from West Branch north to the Straits, you could find another with the same claim.

With the present trend, the years will be preciously few before someone is claiming the last wolf in the United States...or North America.

The wolf senses this. He knows that each year he must range through greater and greater distances to find the tracks of others of his kind. And if, in a winter night of silence and bitter cold, he throws back his head and howls, suddenly and unreasonably, he does not always expect an answering note.

Curious, yet fearful and puzzled because the changes men make on the face of this earth are beyond the range of his understanding, he waits in the cover and he watches.

BOOK TWO The Bears

VIII

THE GREAT WHITE BEAR

THE edge of the Arctic polar cap is an indefinite, changing boundary. The broken pan-ice and the new bergs alternate with stretches of open water and the formations are forever shifting with the seasons and the wind. Silence is almost unknown in this place of ice and ice-like water. Clashing winds scream across great barren distances. Massive bergs grind together in the waves and the floes crash and crack with thundering reports as new mountains of ice fall from the pack to the ocean.

But here, in a world of desolation and bitter cold, there is life.

Tiny, shrimp-like krill swarm close to the ice, seeking salt-free water. Schools of fish of all sizes, colors and shapes follow and feed off the krill. The little ringed seals dot the sea as they follow the fish, sometimes joined by great bearded seals or even herds of walruses.

And here, too, there is death.

Hidden in the jagged forest of pan-ice, blending himself into the world he knew, a giant bear lay motionless. He was a slender creature, nearly ten feet long, with a large neck and a small head. His yellow-white fur was very dense and covered even the soles of his feet. Like the indiscernible drifting of a berg, he made his way through crags of ice, his head lifting occasionally, his jaws parting slightly and showing a black mouth and tongue between deadly white fangs. His snaky head was thrust forward, his rear legs trailing behind as he pulled himself with his front paws.

Fifty yards away, across a short stretch of open water, a ringed seal lay on the ice. The bear crept a little closer, then watched and waited. He could see the breathing hole just beside the seal and he knew this would be a difficult stalk for any wild hunter. At the last bit of cover before the water he lay still.

The seal had been in the open for nearly a minute. With startling suddenness it flipped over and disappeared through the air hole to feed once more in the gray depths beneath the white world.

The bear had been waiting for this. He rose suddenly to all fours, his shoulders almost five feet above the ice, trotted quickly to the edge and slid into the water. He was very nearly as large as a Kodiak brown bear. He weighed more than 1200 pounds. And yet the slight splash he made was lost in the sound of wind and complaining ice. He swam easily with powerful dog-like strokes and waited at the opposite edge. Seals have to breathe. The bear knew this.

For nearly ten minutes he floated in the water, his head held just high enough to watch the breathing hole. There was a flash of movement. Instantly, he sank below the surface.

In water like liquid ice he swam under the bottom of the floe and waited at the outlet of the breathing hole. If the ice had been thinner he would have made a scratching noise and startled the seal into diving into his reach. Here he could only wait. Seconds went by like years as he floated beneath the ice. Time ticked slowly off in his lungs.

At the last possible moment, when he was about to go back up for air and try again, he caught a glimpse of the seal coming down. His massive paws steadied themselves for a back-snapping blow.

Just then a surge of water moved him sideways, an undersea wave came from the constantly-changing ice-pack. He twisted and swung desperately, but the seal was through his grasp and disappearing in the dimness. Furious and writhing with frustration, his lungs doubling up inside him, he fought his way out from beneath the ice and up to the surface. Climbing back onto the pan-ice he stood still with his white flanks heaving and his black mouth gasping for air.

After a few minutes he began threading his way on through the crags, quartering away from the edge of the cap that rose like a mountain range in the distance. He was very hungry and he was hunting frantically now. His long neck swung back and forth as he padded on. His eyes searched the white wasteland for movement, his nose tested the air for scent. In a world of grumbling and complaining ice, his ears were almost useless. He swam the open stretches and walked the floes, searching out his own domain just as a jaguar in an equatorial jungle searches his. For wild hunters in all climes are much alike. They hunt with hunger and loneliness, they master the skill of the stalk or the chase to a degree no human could understand. It is part of the scheme of Nature that predators have just a little more patience than the species on which they prey.

The polar bear came suddenly to the edge of a great expanse of open water. He stood erect with his head high. More than a mile away, in another clutter of bergs and floes, there was movement. His nostrils caught the scent of living creatures and instantly he slipped into the water. If the distance had been twenty miles he still would not have hesitated. The great white bears are probably the most powerful swimmers of all creatures that walk on four legs. He knew no fear of the open ocean. He knew only that hunger had become a living, biting thing within him that had to be silenced.

He'd been born to hunger and he'd carried his burden alone. On a day early one ten-month winter, a big sow bear had sought out a field of pressure ice where packed snow covered great caverns beneath the slabs. She had burrowed far down beneath the surface and the ice-filled wind had promptly sealed the shaft. Among polar bears only pregnant sows hibernate. In the world above her den, the sun had gone down below the horizon to stay, the long Arctic night had begun.

In January, beneath a dark fifty-below-zero world of constant blizzard and driving snow, the bear that now hunted alone had been born with one brother, a hairless ten-inch creature that weighed less than two pounds and lived only by snuggling in the shaggy fur of his mother. In March, with longer and longer stretches of daylight seeping dimly through the snow, the bears had broken out to the world above. Immediately the cubs had been weaned and the lessons of staying alive had begun. For well over a year the mother had taught them how to hunt and how to kill. Then one day in June she had turned on them and driven them off. A two-year cycle was complete. She was ready to mate again.

At this time, the bear that now swam across the open ocean had weighed over two hundred pounds and had been capable of looking after himself. For more than three years he'd lived and hunted alone, avoiding the other white bears entirely. Then, and each of the years since, he'd mated. But courtship had lasted only a few days each June. Very nearly all of his life had been spent alone. He'd covered great distances in his wanderings. Some years he'd floated southward far below the Arctic Circle, riding the ice down through the Bering Strait. He had spent summers on the mountains of Bering Sea islands, digging puffins and eating grass like the brownies. But always, when the freeze-up came, he had headed north again, seeking the world he knew best, the world for which he'd been created.

Yes, he'd lived his life alone, just as he now swam alone across the rolling ice-studded sea toward more promising hunting. His legs, jointed differently from those of other bears, swung sideways in wide circles as he swam, like a human swimmer doing the breast-stroke.

He was close enough now to identify the movement he'd seen from the pan-ice. He slowed his speed in the water and began circling cautiously. This was going to be a far more dangerous kind of hunting than seal-stalking.

A herd of walruses sprawled lazily on the ice. They were massive creatures, weighing up to a ton and a half. Their thick brown hides, warty and wrinkled, seemed almost hairless. Some of the big bulls were twelve feet long with three-foot, yellow-white tusks that gave them a look of age and dignity.

Many of the walruses were feeding, sliding from the ice to dive a hundred yards to the ocean floor and dig clams with the great tusks, shoveling them into a stomach the size of a wash-tub. Then back up to the air and ice they'd float to heave their mighty bulks back on the floes and sleep off the heavy feeding.

As lazy and inoffensive as these giant creatures looked, the polar bear knew well how quickly their temperament would change when he attacked. Two things he'd learned in years of hunting: on the ice he could out-dodge the walruses and hold his own against the whole herd if he had to; in the water he wouldn't have a chance. He circled around to climb up far out of sight of the herd. Then he began once more his painfully slow, belly-flat stalk, his neck snaking ahead, his hind legs dragging behind.

He had already picked his prey. At the edge of the herd, on a floe that rested against the main berg, a female lay asleep. Her three-months-old pup was nearby, a four-foot-long baby of perhaps a hundred and twenty pounds—curious and playful, wandering farther and farther from the safety of the herd.

The big white bear was capable of killing a full-grown walrus. But this might be a long and difficult task and he would never be able to drag the carcass away fast enough to escape the attack of the herd. His little eyes were fastened intently on the pup as he crept along the edge of the berg. An upright slab of pressure ice gave him his last bit of cover. He waited there and picked his moment. Then he doubled his legs beneath him and went down the slope of the berg and across the floe at a full run.

The young walrus turned only at the last minute. It gave only one cry before it died.

The mother walrus woke, waddled about to face him and blew loudly through her nostrils. He snarled at her, then clamped his jaws on the pup's neck and began dragging it across the floe toward the berg. The female was roaring and bellowing steadily as she started to follow. Another walrus, farther down

He snarled at the mother walrus, then clamped his jaws on the pup's neck and began dragging it across the floe.

the shore of the berg, took up the cry. Then another and another, coming toward the scene of the kill with the slow, waddling, sliding motion that was, for them, desperate haste.

The bear backed up to the edge of the berg, jerked the carcass across and braced himself for the pull up the slope to the fields of pressure ice. He was no longer worried about the outcome. In his own mind he had already succeeded. Even with the burden of his kill he could outdistance any walrus. His only thought now was to get far enough away from the angry creatures to feed, to rip apart the young hide and satisfy the torture in his stomach. The entire herd was following him. The bellowing roar sounded exactly like the baying of a pack of foxhounds, magnified to the volume of thunder and echoing from the distant bluffs of the ice cap.

But the white world, once more, is a place of constant change, a land of pressures and stresses that even men have not fathomed, far beyond the understanding or control of the creatures who live there. Gusts of wind had been rocketing in from the ocean to the cap. A rising undersea current, caused by the steady settling of sections of the pack, had been cutting into this iceberg from beneath, just as a river forms its bed in land or rock. Suddenly a series of sharp cracking noises exploded above the roar of the herd. The slabs at the edge of the pressure ice shook, then parted abruptly.

The bear hurried on with his kill. He did not yet realize that he was trapped with the herd on a floe no more than a hundred yards wide and three hundred yards long. He backed steadily toward the security of the pressure ice.

All at once he dropped the pup and turned about. A widening stretch of open water lay before him.

For an instant he considered swimming with his kill for the safety of the main berg. His nerve failed him. He knew how quickly the herd could catch him in the water. He considered leaving the pup and swimming for his own safety. The great void of hunger inside him rebelled.

He waited too long and the decision was made for him. He was going to have to fight it out on this little island of ice.

First, he flipped the baby walrus on its back, tore it open and began gorging himself. Each time he ripped away a great chunk of the hot meat and gulped it down, he lifted his head to check the position of the attacking herd. He crammed himself through the last possible split-second.

Then, with a great roar, he charged the nearest walrus.

It raised its head to meet his rush. Like plowshares beaten into swords, the long tusks that had been used for clam-digging now thrust and flashed in the air. But the bear dodged to the side, then swung in from behind with his heavy paws smashing like axes, striking at the massive neck, trying to break the bones beneath the three-inch hide.

The walrus turned, unhurt, and lunged at him. He leaped aside and attacked another, twisting nimbly past the tusks and then slashing at the side with both fang and claw. On down the waving line of the advancing herd he went, a raging demon of destruction, tearing at the slow-moving giants.

But the herd came on. Their tusks glistened, lined in formation like the spears of an ancient army. They packed together tightly as they dragged their weight nearer. The lone animals that had been good targets for the bear's attacks dropped back to the safety of the battle line. The row of tusks advanced.

The bear had been fighting for his kill. Now he was fighting for his life.

His dodging and slashing ended abruptly as the solid line of giants edged toward him. He backed away to get speed and his weight behind him, then attacked, a white mass of fury, a snarling terror that opened great horrible slashes in the mass of immovable flesh that opposed him. All along the row he raged, defying the array of tusks. He was a creature gone mad with fear. He took insane chances, fought a fight of madness.

But the walrus battle line held firm. Fighting the great fin-feet was like matching skill and speed against the pressure of mountains of ice. Bit by bit, they crowded him back toward the edge of the floe. At least fifty of them, more than fifty tons of weight, packed tightly together.

The inevitable happened. The ice gave way. With a flurry of staccato reports, like a string of firecrackers going off, the floe shattered beneath the massed herd. The little raft of ice where the bear stood at bay dipped down, balanced a split second, then flipped on over, catapulted him out into the crowded churning mass of splintered ice and walruses.

In the water there was no real battle. They killed him quickly. His jaws slashed and snapped constantly, but his paws were useless now. Almost leisurely, the mammoth bull walruses smashed his bones between them, ripped his hide apart with their tusks. Even when he was a shapeless, lifeless thing they kept after him.

Suddenly a walrus bellowed. Instantly, others took up the cry.

This was no roar of triumph. The herd was scrambling desperately up the edge of the main berg now. The commotion and the blood in the water had attracted newcomers to the scene—the water-wolves of the Arctic, the giant dolphins men call killer-whales. The blunt-snouted twenty-foot shapes came through the ocean at express-train speed and drove into the crowded walrus herd, the whites of their bellies flashing as they ripped and tore. The walruses made no attempt at fighting back. Their only chance lay in getting up on the berg and they jammed its shoreline, hoisting their chests on the ice and scrambling away from the water.

At least a dozen of them failed to make it. Their cries ended abruptly, the killers tore them apart and bolted them down in a very few seconds. One big bull was thrown completely out of the water by a killer that smashed into him from beneath. Another walrus climbed onto a segment of the broken ice floe. The killers battered it apart to get at him.

The movement in the water ceased, the struggle died away. The killers patrolled the berg for a few minutes, their high dorsal fins just breaking the surface. Then, as abruptly as they had come, they were gone. A cloud of red spread in the water, slowly dropping away as the berg floated on out to sea.

For at least a half hour the herd huddled together on the ice. Then, bit by bit, the fear drained out of them. Most of the walruses sprawled out and went back to sleep. A few began searching for clams again, diving the length of a football field, down through the icy water.

IX

LORD OF THE MOUNTAINS

One

IT was late afternoon and the shadows of the Rockies had already fallen across a grass-covered floor where beef-cattle grazed in silence and contentment. It was early autumn. A chill had come into the air the instant the sun had slipped down behind the high forbidding crags of rock. There was no wind. Only a faint drone of birdsong broke the hush that hung over the valley.

In the cover of a juniper thicket a bear lay in wait. He was a huge creature, a mountain of fur and muscle, and yet the lacework of branches covered him so completely that the meadow birds were roosting without fear at the thicket's edge. His deep-set little eyes were fastened intently on a young steer who had wandered some distance from the main body of the herd.

This bear had never attacked cattle before. He felt, at that moment, very much like a human being who has been driven by desperation to attempt a bank robbery must feel. He had been lying in ambush for several hours and yet uneasiness still clouded his determination to go ahead and make his kill. He had no fear of the cattle, no fear of any creature he had ever encountered in his lifetime. But like most wild animals, he felt an inner dread of the unknown, a troubling uncertainty when doing anything he had not previously done.

Suddenly indecision was driven from the bear's mind. The steer that had slowly been drifting nearer and nearer to the thicket stopped and lifted its head from the grass. In surprise, it stared dumbly at the far-off herd. Then it moved into a lumbering gait that resembled a trot and started back.

With an explosive snapping and splintering of branches, the bear broke his way free of the cover and hurried across the open. The frightened steer had barely forced his legs into an awkward run when the foot-long paws with four-inch claws and a half-ton of weight behind them smashed down on his hindquarters and broke his back.

A feeling of surprise overshadowed the apprehension in the bear's mind as he stood above the writhing, dying animal. He had never before known such easy prey as this. The slowest whitetail deer would have been able to escape a charge made at that distance. No elk would have allowed itself to be ambushed so easily.

He fastened his jaws on the neck of the steer and wrenched and twisted. The animal's convulsive movements ended.

The bear looked out across the grasslands at the other cattle. They were milling about uneasily. Sensing that he should leave this disturbed place, the giant bear clamped his teeth once more in his kill, then started toward the side of the nearest mountain. Sometimes he dragged the steer behind him. Sometimes he picked it up and carried it bodily.

More than a mile away, in a tight hidden spot where a canyon dwindled into a mere gorge, he dropped his kill and ripped open its stomach with a single slash of his great claws. There, in seclusion, he fed.

Two line-riders trotted their horses along the edge of the cover that bordered the valley floor, seeking out strays to drive them back to the herd before nightfall. One of the horses shied and tried to turn back at the edge of the juniper thicket. While calming him, the rider suddenly noticed the trampled grass, freshly painted with blood.

He dismounted and handed the reins to his companion. The trail where the steer had been dragged away was easy to follow.

116

On the far side of the thicket, the grass was stunted and broken with bare stretches of sandy earth. Tracks were clear and distinct. The man knelt beside them for a second, then hurried back.

"Grizzly!" he told the other rider, as he pulled a lever-action rifle from his saddle sheath and stuffed cartridges into his pocket. "Get word back to the ranch to get the dogs up here."

The other man stared at him, then turned to look at the mountains, already dimming with the forbidding gloom of twilight. "You going up there? Now? Alone?"

"He won't get too far." The man with the rifle ran back to the spot where he'd found the tracks, then moved slowly on, following a trail of trampled brush and bloodstains.

The mounted man watched him disappear over the crest of a ridge. Then he urged both horses into a gallop and raced directly across the pastureland.

The light in the air was failing when the great bear of the mountains rose to his feet and dragged the remains of the steer into a clump of short, wiry growth that bordered the ravine. He took the time to cover the carcass completely with branches, dead leaves and a layer of earth. Then he climbed the steep bank, pulled himself over the brink of a ledge and headed back into the mountains, moving through the uneven, difficult terrain at a pace that was steady and yet unhurried.

He was an impressive creature. His blackish-gray fur rose above and behind his shoulders like the hair of a frightened housecat, tipped with silver. His head was large and wide; his face and muzzle long and narrow.

His confidence and his dignity were obvious in his gait and manner. He never wandered aimlessly about merely through curiosity, as a black bear does. He never fought loud but half-hearted battles with other bears or romped and rolled about in the autumn grass. When he made his way through the mountains, his walk was ponderous and yet somehow as agile as a puma's pace. Nearly always, he moved in a straight line, direct and purposeful. The big mountain lions stepped from the pathway at his approach, slinking off to the safety of clefts in the rock to snarl and spit their hatred. Black bears scurried into the trees at his coming. Coyotes trotted quickly toward the security of the underbrush. For the gigantic silvertipped grizzly was king of this land—largest, strongest and deadliest of all the creatures that lived their lives throughout the barren crags or in the thick forest below. And when he walked through the cover all movement and noises in the thickets ceased, all living things held their breath until he had passed.

His life had had its beginning in the mid-winter den of a sow silvertip who, a half-year before, had given up her solitary way of life for a few weeks of keeping company with a boar grizzly. During this short mating period the grizzly pair would have appeared extremely affectionate to an observer. They had grazed with their noses close together, sometimes hugging and pawing each other. But in less than a month they had both tired of this relationship. After a few days of finding his mate sullen and unapproachable, the boar bear had gone his own lonely way.

Grizzlies are almost as small at birth as black bears and they mature twice as slowly, usually requiring ten years to gain their full weight. For this reason most sow silvertips mate every third year instead of every second. This gives a grizzly two and a half years of childhood.

Every day of it had been needed. Keeping himself fed is a tremendous task for any large mammal in a state of transition from carnivore to grass-eater. Staying alive, to the puma, means becoming a successful stalker and slayer of deer. Staying alive, to the timber wolves of the barrens, means learning to pull down caribou efficiently. But the grizzly is no longer a highly-specialized predator. Occasionally, he may overtake a sick or crippled elk or deer, ambushing his prey or surprising it in a swift and deadly charge. Once in a while he may come across a fawn that is not yet old enough to escape him.

Sometimes the mother bear and her cub had dug out ground squirrels and mice. But this was a long hard task and its reward was never more than a few mouthfuls. When first coming out

118

of hibernation they'd scouted their range for the carcasses of winter-killed animals and fed on the decaying flesh.

Most of the time, they'd been forced to be vegetarians. In the early summer they'd dug roots and grazed like cows on the hillside, swallowing tons of grass. Even before the blueberries were ripe they'd begun moving through the patches and stripping the bushes, gulping down the leaves along with the fruit.

The lessons the great silvertip had learned from his mother dealt only with finding food. Grizzlies had no enemies to fear or evade in these mountains.

The giant bear had been more than twenty years old when civilization spread to the valleys below his domain. Men on horseback had driven cattle into the grasslands one spring, visited them only occasionally throughout the summer and then herded them off in the fall.

For three full years the big grizzly had watched the invaders from the heights of his mountain fortress and felt neither fear nor anger. Sometimes, when the cattle were gone, he'd roamed across the range drinking in the strong scent of beef that had been instilled in the earth during the hot months. He'd sniffed the shiny new barbwire fences curiously, investigated the worn paths made by thousands of hooves. But never until this year had he preyed on cattle.

This year an early spring had followed a mild winter. Very few deer and elk had perished in the cold months and the bear's usual meals of carrion were not to be found in the mountains. The extremely light snowfall had not turned the streams into great rushing torrents, as always before. Summer had come early, hot and very dry. Grass and ferns were stunted and browned. No fruit appeared on the berry bushes.

When autumn comes, a lean bear is a desperate one, for the layers of fat are life itself during the half-sleep of winter. The gigantic silvertip had slipped quietly into the thicket that bordered the grasslands. His hunger had conquered his dread of new experience.

The grizzly kept on the move throughout most of the night.

Just as the moon was going down he made his way along a narrow ledge, high above the timber line, and then stopped to turn back and face the valley, far below. He listened for several minutes, scented the wind that was dying as dawn approached. Then he turned and made his way deep into the rocks and settled down, facing the opening.

The giant bear slept soundly until well past noon. When the sun swung into the southwest the light reached into his hiding place and he became partway awake, stretching with pleasure as his long fur and his great body soaked up the great warmth. But when the sun slipped on past the peaks he lifted himself to his feet and climbed back out into the open.

He stepped on along the ledge until it widened and the steep wall above became the rounded crest of a ridge. Here he found sunlight once again. He stopped, reared high on his hind legs to look for movement on the vast slope below, then sat down abruptly, relaxing in the luxurious brightness. After a few minutes he began licking and grooming each crease and corner of his fur.

All too soon, the shadow of distant and still higher mountains reached the slope and warmth left the thin air immediately. The grizzly pushed up to his feet and started on down the ridge, his weight forcing his legs into a trot.

He was hungry now. He was heading directly for the little canyon where he'd cached the remnants of his kill.

Hidden in the rocks that overlooked the cover where he'd finally found the butchered steer, the hunter twisted his cramped body slightly and rubbed circulation back into his chilled hands.

He'd been lying in this spot since mid-morning. The steer had been carried much farther than he'd believed possible and darkness had forced him to give up attempting to trail. He'd spent an autumn night in the wild without blankets and he'd slept very little. Since noon, he'd been fighting to stay awake.

The hunter was wondering now just what he'd do if nothing happened before darkness came again. Waiting at this spot through the night would be futile. Starting back for the valley in darkness with a raider grizzly somewhere in these mountains was something he did not even wish to consider.

The hunter was just about to get to his feet and start for the grasslands while there was still time enough to get through. But suddenly, the canyon seemed strangely hushed. The chatter of birds in the brush had cut out abruptly.

For less than a hundred yards away there came the unmistakable sound of branches springing together after they'd been parted.

He eased back the hammer on his rifle, then lay perfectly still.

Darkness was only minutes away when the giant bear stalked up the narrow ravine and forced his bulk into the thicket. He sniffed the mound where his kill was buried, then lifted his head and tested the air. Something was wrong. This spot had been disturbed. He roared his anger loudly.

Suddenly his left rear haunch seemed to be torn apart and in the same instant the flash and crack of a rifle came from the opposite canyon wall. The grizzly had never been hunted or fired at before. His dread of the unknown sent him charging on down the draw at a full run. The rifle exploded twice more behind him.

Dodging around the boulders and larger trees, smashing his way directly through the thickets, the bear raced back toward the high country. There were no sounds of pursuit as he dashed out through the canyon mouth, across a small valley and up a long slope of rock and shale, each heavy step leaving a small avalanche behind. But his pace did not slow. Panic and desperation spurred him on through the pine woods that were tangled with blowdowns and deadfalls, into the belt of scrub and finally out above the timber line where he felt the familiar rock beneath his feet, cold and hard.

The absolute blackness of a cloudy night had closed down on the mountains when the grizzly finally slid into the security of a cavern formed by tumbled rock slabs, an old hibernation den he had used several winters before. For a long time he rested flat on his side, waiting for strength to come back to his body. Then he raised his head and tried to reach the wounded haunch with his tongue.

The bullet had not crippled him. It had merely ripped through flesh and hide, opening a great tear in his coat. A thin layer of fat had puffed out and closed the cut. It was bleeding very little now. But the pain was intense and throbbing.

The grizzly did not move from this hiding place throughout the entire night. He was not disturbed again but he did not sleep. The torture of his wound was becoming unbearable. He snapped and slashed at his own flesh.

When morning came he crept warily out of the rocks and worked his way down to drink from a white-water mountain stream. But his wound had caused a burning inside him that water could not cool. He stretched out full length where the sun slanted into the creekside growth and lay still again. But there was no comfort in the bright warmth now.

The hound pack arrived at the summer-range camp in the middle of the afternoon, too late to start a bear hunt that day. The man who had wounded the raider grizzly fed them himself and looked them over.

These dogs were not his, of course. They were owned by the cattle company that employed him. They were pets of no man, but rather working animals whose talents were indispensable. The men who would follow them on the hunt in the morning had a deep respect for the skill of these hounds, and there was a great deal more dignity in that respect than in lavish affection, such as a city-dweller's pet might receive. These dogs cared nothing for fondling or petting. The chase was their only love.

When they ran in full cry and felt the sharp scent of a bear or a big cat in their nostrils, every muscle and nerve of their bodies would come to life. Now they lay about the camp listlessly. Long ears and dropping jowls gave them an appearance of sadness and half-closed eyes made them look sleepy.

*   *   *

Flies had swarmed into the thicket throughout the entire day to light on the festering tear in the grizzly's hide. Each attempt at swatting them away had brought new heights of torture to his body. By evening he could no longer lie still.

He pushed to his feet and trotted hurriedly on down the creekbed, shaking convulsively from time to time as if to throw off the pain. He was moving back toward the low country but he paid little attention to direction. He smashed his way savagely through the stream growth, growled repeatedly to himself as he worked through the hills toward the grasslands. His dread of the thing that had wounded him was smothered by pain.

The great bear of the mountains killed six more steers that night. He mutilated them horribly, but he did not feed. He rampaged on across the pastureland. When a fence blocked his passage he tore at the posts, snapping them cleanly or pulling them completely out of the ground. All through the valley he raged, seeking revenge for his suffering.

At dawn he instinctively headed back for his mountains. The sun had not yet come up when he heard the first sounds of pursuit. Hounds were singing on his trail.

The grizzly had never been chased before. The baying that was steadily growing louder behind him brought no fear to his mind. He turned in his tracks, stood still and listened for some time. Then he seized upon the hound voices as merely another outlet for his rage. He actually charged back to attack the pursuing pack.

When a common black bear turns at bay, it usually attempts the impossible task of fighting all the hounds at once, rearing up on its hind legs and swinging in all directions. Not a grizzly. The big silvertips invariably defend themselves by fighting an offensive battle, singling out one dog at a time for their attack.

The grizzly waited until the leaders of the pack swerved to either side and began circling him for the fight. Then he picked a large bluetick hound who was already dodging in and snapping at his haunches. With a deadly quickness that seemed impossible for a creature his size, the bear smashed down on the dog and left him screaming and flopping about in the grass with a broken neck.

As the grizzly turned to defend himself once more he felt hound teeth sinking into his legs. He spun around and his great arms whipped through the air. One unlucky hound kept his teeth in bear-hide a split-second too long. A glancing blow sent him cartwheeling through the air, yelping. But he pushed himself up from the grass and trotted back to the fight.

The dogs at his back leaped in and slashed, then dodged away quickly when he whirled to face them.

This hound pack had brought bears to bay before, fought them successfully before. The dogs ringed about the big silvertip and kept moving. The ones at his back leaped in and slashed, attempting to hamstring him, then dodged away quickly when he whirled to face them. The instant he turned, the hounds on the other side moved in for the attack. Faced with a pack as skilled as this, a black bear would have been helpless.

But the grizzly merely singled out another hound and charged after it. The dog turned and ran, but the bear kept up the chase, forcing himself to ignore the others, who were harassing his sides and hind legs, fighting the impulse to turn in his tracks and flail at his tormentors. Even when one of the dogs kept his teeth in the grizzly's loose, shaggy skin and let his weight drag, the giant silvertip kept up his chase of the hound he'd first singled out. He caught the dog after a run of perhaps fifty yards and pinned it against the ground. It rolled on its back, snapping and kicking. One blow from the grizzly's paw disemboweled it.

Then the bear turned and fought the pack, slapped the hounds from him as though they were flies. He was just about to pick and kill another hound when he caught a glimpse of movement on the slope below. Men on horseback were racing to join the fight. The grizzly's success in the short, furious battle had left him with no fear of the hounds. But he reared up on his hind legs for a better look at this new danger.

Then his stomach exploded. A white-hot bolt of pain burst through his insides. He recognized the sound of gunfire as the thing that had hurt him before.

Terror came over him once again. He lumbered away from the horses, even forced his tortured body into a trot. A rifle blasted once more and a bullet smashed into the flesh beside the day-old wound, but strength came from his fear and he kept on going. The hound pack raged on both sides of him all through the open stretches. The mounted men kept coming on and the sound of a rifle echoed several times more. But none of the shots touched the fleeing grizzly.

He left the dogs behind the minute he reached the canyons, but he kept on running until he was above the timber line. Then he moved at a steady walk, forcing each step over the terrible pain in his stomach. He headed directly for the far peaks, headed for country that was beyond his previous range. His only thought was to leave the thing that had hurt him far behind.

When night came he was across the highest part of the range and followed the barren slopes down toward a cluster of pine-covered foothills. The torture inside him had increased to such heights that he slashed constantly at his own flesh. His temper had reached a pitch where he would attack and destroy any living creature he happened to encounter.

Two

In a thick cluster of wild strawberry bushes, midway in sandy ridges that climbed like a staircase from the floor of a valley to the foothills, a number of black bears were feeding.

These shaggy creatures were as noisy and as varied as a similar group of people at a picnic. Occasionally a cub would be cuffed by an older bear, especially if he was encroaching on his elder's feeding spot. But even when the cuffed youngster's mother came to his defense, the squabble would be brief and half-hearted.

Basically, black bears are peaceful animals. Even the few bullies in the group, who sometimes blustered and threatened smaller and more timid animals, seemed to be doing so in fun. The arguments that took place were not serious. The spasmodic grunting growls were not sounds of deadliness. If a human observer had been hidden in the growth of the ridge, the bears would have appeared to him very much like a pack of giant puppies, feeding and at play.

But suddenly one of the bears raised its head and tested the air. There was no wind and just the suggestion of a strange scent drifted down from above. Other bears in the group caught the scent. Uneasiness spread over them like a cloud shading the sun.

Out of the cover of the ridge above, a giant form came into

sight, hesitated just a second in the open. This creature was colored dark gray and wore a stiff brush of mane that was tipped with silver. Its nose was long and pointed. It stared at the group of black bears, then hurried forward.

Most of the bears had never seen a grizzly before. The gigantic silvertips were scarce in these mountains and the few that still existed almost never came down to the ridge country. But even the cubs sensed fear in the scent of the stranger as it lurched along the ridge toward the berry patch.

A wise old black bear grunted a warning and then turned and trotted quickly away. Mothers called their cubs and herded them off through the brush. As though Nature had flipped a switch, the berry patch was vacated. But one young male stood perfectly still, frozen with fear, unable to move.

The grizzly did not even break its stride. The silvertip hump came through the bushes just as the high dorsal fin of a killer whale slices the water. Its face was expressionless. Its jaws parted only when it lunged. The scream of the smaller black bear dwindling into a bubbling sound as he thrashed and twisted in the bushes like a freshly-killed chicken, his throat torn in half.

The grizzly feared no reprisals. He did not as much as glance in the direction of the fleeing blackies as he lay full length beside the carcass of his slaughtered cousin, ripped open the stomach and fed half-heartedly.

Deep in the cover, one old black bear watched for a moment, then turned and hurried on. The wild was no longer at peace. A deadly terror had come to the ridge country.

Several hours later, when night had closed down completely, the old black bear stood at the edge of the bottom-land cover and stared tightly over the fields of a small wilderness farm. The lights of the house gleamed warmly a few hundred yards away, pin-points of brightness in a world of autumn chill and night. A slight wind was beginning to stir and the black bear tested its direction carefully, then circled far to the left before cutting across the open.

Flat on his belly, he snaked his way across the very edge of the farmhouse yard and entered a clump of apple trees. The scent of dogs and men reached him on the rising breeze, but no sound of movement came from the house. He lowered his head to the ground and began searching for windfall fruit.

A half-hour passed and he found only one small dried apple. He had rooted out the entire area. His nose had tested every square inch of the ground. The apples had been gathered very recently.

The black bear watched the house once more, listening carefully, waiting for several minutes. Then he rose on his hind legs, gripped the smooth bark of one of the trees and started up.

Moving out on the first branch and bracing himself, he began shaking the tree as silently and carefully as possible. An apple thudded against the ground, then another. He shook the branch harder and the fruit rained down. But the limb began cracking beneath his weight and he clung to the trunk once more.

Suddenly, on the far side of the house, the stillness was shattered by the loud baying of a hound. Another took up the cry. Then the sound of an entire pack, straining at their kennel leashes and shrieking with impatience, tore the night wide open. A door slammed.

The bear hit the ground, bounding lightly in spite of his bulk and weight, and shot like a rifle bullet out of the orchard and across the open fields. The thick muscles in his legs drove at the ground beneath him, again and again. He smashed into the growth at the far end of the clearing and bore straight toward the far end of the valley, running hard for the security of the ridges that were his home.

A man's shout rang out in the darkness behind him. The impatient, demanding cries of the hounds changed to yelps of pure excitement as they were freed. The pack burst into the orchard, screamed the discovery. Then their voices steadied. The full cry of a wide-open chase echoed completely across the valley. The driving voices came nearer and nearer.

The black bear forced his bulk through the thickness at an unbelievable speed. But in cover this tight, the advantage lay with the smaller hounds. The song of the chase was rapidly growing louder in the brushland behind him. Desperation and panic twisted through his stomach.

But this bear had been hunted before. He circled about, out of the thicker brush, then raced for at least a quarter-mile along the edge of the cleared land.

He had put a breathing space between himself and the hound pack and he used it well. Circling and back-tracking, he worked his way to the banks of a little stream that came down from the mountains to feed the valley's river. He had no fear of the rapids as he moved upstream through the racing water where neither hounds nor men could follow. His weight kept his footing firm and steady on the rocks.

The hound voices cut out in the night air. When they sounded again, there was only the uncertain baying of dogs attempting to work out a bad loss. Finally, all sounds of the chase ended and silence surged back.

High up in the ridges, the wary old black bear listened carefully. Fear had left him. He was sure of himself once again. In his satisfaction at outwitting hounds he had forgotten entirely his hunger for apples.

He began making his way back toward the wilderness end of the valley. He was in no particular hurry now. A combination of wanderlust and curiosity was his guiding feeling and he kept on the move throughout most of the night.

He slept through the daylight hours, waking only when the late afternoon sunlight slanted into the thicket where he'd made his bed. Like a man who has not yet had his morning coffee, he walked stiffly and grunted crossly as he made his way down to the creek. He drank for several minutes, then set out moving upstream.

Whatever the wild land could offer would have to do for his dinner tonight. He was not yet ready to risk another chase.

He had lived a long time. And although, like all black bears, his every action appeared clownish, his years had given him wisdom.

He weighed nearly five hundred pounds now, but he'd weighed less than eight ounces the January day a hibernating mother had given him birth—blind and hairless and toothless, like a little caricature of a bulldog with only the suggestion of legs and ears. For many months, life had been easy for the bear family. The mother had dozed on and the cubs had known where to find milk.

In spring, they'd left the den. The cubs had weighed about four pounds then and already sported a coat of black down-like hair. The mother bear had looked as bulky as she had before hibernating. This was because a bear's layers of winter fat are spongy and porous. A bear begins shrinking only after coming out of hibernation. The mother bear had had no appetite at first. She'd nibbled half-heartedly at the early grass. Within two weeks she'd been lean and practically starving and life had become a constant search for food. Following her, the cubs had taken enough time out from their romping and their mischief to learn to hunt mice and ground squirrels, to dig for roots, to strip berry bushes, to fish, to hunt down such delicacies as honey or the flesh of winter-killed elk, rotting and alive with maggots.

At any suggestion of danger in the forest world, a hoarse grunt from the mother bear had been the signal for the cubs to go sprinting into the tree tops. If they'd hesitated in the slightest they'd been cuffed roughly. At the ends of the branches, where no larger predator could follow, they'd sometimes waited for hours while their mother had investigated the surrounding cover. If a coyote or a lynx had been lying in wait, it had retreated rapidly before the sow bear's anger.

The cubs had hibernated with their mother only one winter. The following spring she'd started to show very little interest in them. The mating urge had come back and become stronger than maternal feelings. One day in June, she'd given the danger signal and sent them hurrying into the trees. They'd remained there until hunger forced them down, but they'd never seen their mother again.

The cubs had lived together for another year, then separated to seek out mates for the first time. As with all species of bears, courtship was brief.

For the largest part of his life, the old black bear who was now grubbing out the river growth had lived alone. He saw others of his kind constantly, when they grouped at some spot where the feeding was good—the ripened fruit of autumn, the spring run of salmon or rainbow trout. But he knew neither the pleasures nor the responsibilities of organized family life, such as that of the wolves or coyotes.

Several days passed before any of the black bears returned to graze on the strawberries. And now, when they fed, they kept well away from the carcass of the young male. They ate in quick, fearful nibbles, raising their heads again and again to sniff the air carefully. There was fear in the very shadows of the ridge-top trees now. The bears spent more time searching the air for grizzly scent than they did feeding or sleeping.

Another young black bear was found slaughtered in a stand of river-bottom jack-pines and that too became a spot to be avoided. Then the silvertipped invader managed to run down a cub. The mother bear died defending it. The odor of decaying flesh spread over the ridge country like some sort of evil mist.

One afternoon the old black bear who had discovered the farmyard apples was crossing an open stretch on the valley floor. He stopped beside the one tree in the clearing, a giant river-bottom oak, and listened intently. Something had moved in the brush ahead. The black bear was about to turn and run when the bushes suddenly parted, forty yards away. With a horrible roar, the great grizzly broke out of the cover and charged in the same motion. His jaws were already spreading in readiness.

If the old black bear had tried to run, he would have lived only a few seconds. Had he tried to fight back his death would have come even more quickly. One thing saved him. In his terror, he instinctively reverted to the lessons he'd received as a cub, nearly twenty years before. Fear made his mind seize upon the only bit of discipline or training he'd ever learned—

his mother's command to climb a tree when danger came. Without thinking about it, he pulled himself up the trunk of the oak.

He made it just in time. The jaws of the grizzly closed with a sound like a sprung steel trap on empty air beneath him. The black bear hurried on into the upper limbs.

It was a long time before he realized that he was safe, that the gray giant who raged about the ground below was not going to follow.

Grizzlies cannot climb trees.

Many hours later, in full darkness, the black bear started down. He lowered himself a few feet along the tree trunk, listened for a long time and scented the night air, then came down a few feet farther before stopping cautiously once more. When he finally reached the ground he bolted directly for the forest's edge and dodged off among the trees, quartering away from the river. His ears and nostrils still regularly tested the cover that surrounded him, but he was no longer really afraid.

He kept on wandering again this night, a dark shadow in a dark forest that would have been invisible to a man a half-dozen paces away. He seldom used the deer runs or river-bed paths as he roamed. Instead, he kept to thick cover.

A little before midnight he came once again to the edge of the cleared farmland. Once more he tested the wind and circled before beginning his stalk of the apple orchard. Once more he crept across a quarter-mile of cleared land on his stomach.

The windfall apples were there this time. Some of them were bruised and rotting and this, by bear standards, added to the flavor. The old black bear swallowed them eagerly, bothering very little with chewing. All of his senses, eyes and ears and nose, were tuned like antenna in the direction of the house. For the night wind was rising, tricky and constantly changing direction as it came through the trees.

Apprehension grew inside him. Several times he started to leave, but the thought of gulping down a few more apples always drew him back to his search of the ground. He stayed just a moment too long.

132

The frantic baying of a hound split the night apart.

The old black bear turned and started out of the orchard at a dead run. But there was no rattle of kennel chains, no choking sounds of dogs straining at their collars. The hounds had been left free to run this night. Before the black bear reached the edge of the field, the pack was upon him.

He turned and fought, rearing up on his hind legs, striking out with all the strength in his great shaggy arms. But these dogs were blooded bearhounds, old and fight-wise and deadly. They raged about him with the precision of skilled teamwork. Each time he bore down on one, his jaws snapping and his claws swinging, others were slashing at his flanks.

The door of the farmhouse opened. The beam of a flashlight stabbed through the dark. The report and flash of a rifle came just as a screaming, spinning piece of lead burned through the air above him. The old black bear made one desperate struggle, freed himself, then turned and started across the field at a full run.

Every bit of his strength and every ounce of his will was concentrated into his dash for the forest. His legs thudded hard against the ground beneath him. He drove hard into a wall of solid brush, smashed his way through with the hound pack still at his heels. There was no time for leaving a tangled trail, no time for circling. He went through the thickness of the forest in a straight run, his weight breaking a path for him. When he reached the river, he had gained only a few yards.

Without hesitating, he splashed in and swam hard for the other shore. As he pulled himself up through the roots and mud of the bank, he knew the dogs were in the water behind him, but he did not look back. A deer run followed along this side of the stream, gave him an open path on which to race at his fullest speed. Behind him, he heard the hound pack bay the discovery at the river bank, heard them driving steadily along the run on his trail.

But he was leaving them behind now. Without thick brush to encumber him, his speed was greater. And he knew he could outlast any dog. He went on at a full run and the fear that had frozen his mind ebbed slowly away.

He had gone nearly a mile along the river and gained several hundred yards on the pursuing dogs when a strange sensation of uneasiness came over him. His pace did not slow, but the intangible feeling that something was wrong grew inside him. Without understanding it, he was afraid again. He knew he was outdistancing the hounds. He knew the hunters with their rifles would still be farther behind. But just the same he felt afraid once more.

Suddenly he realized what was troubling him. Fresh scent marked this deer run. In his concentration on escaping the dogs, he had failed to notice that another bear had come this way very recently, so recently that the spoor was still sharp and tangy. And the old black bear recognized that scent. The giant marauding grizzly was hunting on this runway. At any moment he could come upon the killer from behind.

Instantly, he turned in his tracks and started back. The memory of the big silvertip slaughtering the young male blackie was still fresh in his mind and he felt every bit as much afraid as he had when fighting the hounds. But he had gone no more than thirty yards when he stopped and waited, indecisively.

The hound pack was coming straight toward him, driving hard, singing for blood. He was trapped directly between two deadly enemies. A more terrible fear than he had ever before known in his life grated over him.

Instinctively, he doubled his legs beneath him and bounded far down the steep bank of the river. He was in the water again when the screaming of the dogs seemed to explode just above him. Even in his panic, he listened for the sounds of his pursuers splashing into the river behind him.

But that sound never came. There was no let-up in the baying of the pack. They ran on, straight and hard, knowing and caring for nothing else but the thrill of the chase.

They were running the grizzly's trail now. The old black bear was still in the water when the mounted men went by.

134

By the time he climbed ashore on the far side, the hunt had gone out of hearing.

Late the next afternoon, the old black bear was heading back up through the ridges to feed on berries when he came across the scene where that mis-directed chase had ended. The giant grizzly had refused to run this time. Three hounds lay lifeless and broken among trampled bushes. An entire ridge-bottom swale had been painted bright with blood.

But the hunters had arrived in time. Nothing was left of the grizzly now but a bullet-ridden carcass. Then men had taken the head and the hide.

The coyotes would be here soon, the old black bear knew. The scene of that desperate struggle filled him with dread and he hurried away.

The feeling had left him by the time he reached the berry ridges. More than a dozen other black bears were already at work here and it was obvious from the noise they were making that all members of that wild community knew the thing they had feared no longer existed. The old bear moved among them unhurriedly, selected an untouched clump and began to feed. His nearest neighbors muttered at him and he muttered back, but there was no real threat in the sounds they made. The scene, once more, was that of a human picnic. The cubs played like children. The mothers punished them when necessary and came to their defense with fantastic speed if any other bear attempted punishing them.

The ground was still warm from the sun that was now setting. The bear banquet went on, at peace with a world that was itself at peace.

X

THE NUMBER-ONE TROPHIES

WHAT is the most dangerous beast in the world? The tiger? The lion? The Cape buffalo?

One well-known sportsman, who hunted through very nearly every section of this globe's surface, failed to be misled by the glamor of far-off places. Teddy Roosevelt always made it clear in his writings that he considered the American grizzlies to be superior in fighting ability to any other creature on earth.

Dr. Hornaday, former head of the New York Zoological Park, once composed a list of the animals he considered most dangerous to man. The big brown bear was first; the silvertip, second. The lion was third and the tiger, fourth.

Strangely enough, the men who know the giant bears best, the guides and outfitters of Alaska, seldom agree with this estimate. They point out that there is another animal on this continent, little known and rarely hunted until recent years, whose size and strength are a close second to the brownie's and perhaps even his equal. They remind you that this beast must be pursued in an environment that gives him every advantage and presents every danger to the hunter. They insist that this creature is an uninhibited man-hunter, the only large carnivore in the world who has not been taught fear of man through intensive hunting pressure. They point out that this animal will deliberately stalk and kill men for food, while the brown bear very rarely attacks without being wounded. Merely reaching the range of this beast involves more extreme risk of life than a hunter is likely to encounter in a dozen African safaris or Indian shikars.

When all these facts are considered, it is difficult to dispute the growing opinion that the polar bear, the great white bear of the Arctic ice pack, is the world's most dangerous big-game animal.

Last March 24, several hours after night had closed down over Northern Alaska, the 74th Air Rescue Squadron at Ladd Field was alerted. Another party of ice-bear hunters had failed to return.

Earlier that day, bush-pilot Tommy Richards had flown out of Kotzebue with two hunters. The morning was clear and very bright and Richards had every reason to expect a successful hunt. Two days before, he'd guided a hunter to a record-size bear on this stretch of the ice pack. A week before that, he'd flown three hunters out of Kotzebue and brought them back a short time later with three bear hides.

For several hours he scoured the sunlit ice fields. He checked the site of his most recent kills. Tracks were everywhere but he saw no bears that morning. At noon, he touched down at Point Hope for refueling.

In the early afternoon, he flew out over the ice between Point Hope and Point Barrow. Suddenly, he caught a glimpse of movement below.

A large male polar bear may be four or five feet high at the shoulder, nine to ten feet long and weigh more than 1500 pounds. But from 1000 feet up, he's a minute speck in a vast wasteland of pan-ice and pressure ridges. A successful guide needs the eyes of a falcon in addition to the best dark glasses available. Tommy Richards pointed the bear out to his hunters and then swooped down, attempting to spook the bear into an area of safe ice where a landing would be possible.

The big white beast turned and fled when the plane got too close. He dodged into ice-caverns and hid behind ridges. Several times he slipped into open water and attempted to lose the plane by diving under. Finally, after he'd been chased five miles or more, he stood his ground, rearing up on his hind legs, swinging his great arms and daring the plane to come down and fight. Richards saw a smooth stretch of safe-looking ice a short distance ahead and decided to land.

Setting a plane down on the pack-ice is undoubtedly the riskiest phase of polar-bear hunting. Even the most experienced Arctic pilots can never really be sure the ice is safe. Blowing snow or quick-forming frost can make new ice look like old in a very few minutes.

Suddenly and unexpectedly, Richards' fifteen-thousand-dollar plane dropped through into the twenty-eight degree water of the Arctic Ocean. The ice caught the wing tips and kept the plane from going straight to the bottom, but the cabin filled with water almost at once. One of the hunters got the door open and swam out. The other tried to follow but ice jammed the door and his foot caught in the seat. After a long struggle, he and Richards finally pitched out. Weakened by the shock of the water and weighted down with heavy clothing, all three of the men sank far down before they could fight their way to the surface and drag themselves out on firm ice.

Soaked to the skin, they turned their backs to a knife-like wind that drove the fifteen-below cold completely through them and tried to find a way ashore, but they seemed to be blocked by open leads on all sides. One of the hunters fell through the ice twice more and was nearly pulled under by the fast current. Just before nightfall the two hunters were too exhausted to go any farther. Richards left them by the plane and set out alone, still hoping to find a way ashore and get help back that night. But he got trapped on a berg surrounded by thin new ice.

When absolute darkness came the wind grew stronger and the temperature sank down and down. The three men kept moving constantly, walking back and forth in the shelter of pressure ridges to keep from freezing, praying for the dawn to bring a clear sky.

In the morning, half the small planes in Arctic Alaska took

to the air and winged their way north to join in the search. But the ice-bear guides have a way of looking after their own. It was John Cross, also a Kotzebue bush-pilot, who picked up the stranded men at about eleven that morning and flew them to safety. The two hunters spent some time in hospitals being treated for frostbite. One of them lost a toe. After a brief rest, Tommy Richards was flying bear-hunters out over the ice again.

A short time later another full-scale search was organized. Gene Effler, of Cordova, had gone through the ice in the Point Hope area with one hunter aboard. The two men actually had to swim some distance to another floe. Their rifles were frozen solid and useless. All through the cruel bitter night they played a deadly game of hide and seek with hungry bears among the broken ice ridges. They fell through several times more before morning. After nearly a full day and night on the ice they were found by two other ice-bear guides, Dyton Gilliland and Gordon Kane.

These men, both from Cooper's Landing, had been hunting in the same area as Effler and his passenger the day before, hunting for hides to sell in the fur market, since they'd had no hunters booked at the time. They'd landed and killed a bear, but a frozen carburetor had delayed them in getting off the ice again and they'd lost track of the other plane. It wasn't until they'd landed at Point Hope that night that they'd realized Effler was in trouble.

When Gilliland and Kane first spotted Effler's plane in the water, they understood what had happened. The night wind had blown enough snow away so that the line between thin and safe ice was visible now, but it had been completely hidden when Effler had touched down. Gilliland circled once, certain the two men were dead in the water-filled cabin. Then he swung lower and saw them standing beside an improvised shelter of ice, still strong enough to wave.

The rescue landing was extremely tricky. Gilliland had to come in on the thin ice, keep his speed up to keep from going through, then coast up onto the thicker floe and come to a quick stop. His plane would hold only three men and there wasn't enough daylight left for a trip back out. Kane had to spend a night on the ice while his partner flew the two men into Point Hope, where they received first aid before going on to a hospital.

Rushing up to get in another shot, the hunter slipped and floundered up to his armpits in snow. At that moment the big white beast saw him and charged.

The next morning Gilliland picked up Kane and they started hunting once more. They spotted a bear and Kane stalked him on foot while Gilliland kept track of him from the air. Kane's first bullet smashed into the bear's throat but failed to stop him. As the hunter was rushing up to get in another shot, he slipped and floundered up to his armpits in snow that held him like quicksand. At that moment the big white beast saw him and charged. Aiming carefully, Kane broke each of the bear's front shoulders. But the animal still came on, forcing its bulk over the ice with its hind legs, fighting to stay alive just long enough to get its jaws on the man who was destroying it. Ten feet from Kane, the bear collapsed.

Gilliland and Kane managed to survive the worst ice-bear hunting had to offer. But a short time later, while scouting for a campsite for brownie hunters down on Montague Island, they crashed into a mountain peak and both of them were killed.

One factor that makes the hide of a great white bear the hardest-to-earn item in any trophy room is the deadly Arctic phenomenon known as white-out. Whenever the sun clouds over, up on top of the world, the horizon dissolves. Ice, air and water become one solid milky blur. A good many men have scattered both their planes and themselves over the ice when trapped by weather like this.

Dick McIntyre, Bill Edlund and Captain Albert Scott are well-remembered in Kotzebue for the day last spring when they brought in four bear hides on a single hunt. But less than a week earlier, they'd had a very narrow escape.

Hunting in two planes, they'd sighted a bear some forty miles off the coast. McIntyre and Edlund touched down on the ice while Scott circled above. Just as the plane slid to a stop, a bolt in the rear spring snapped.

Noticing that the weather had suddenly begun closing in, the two men worked frantically to remove the tail ski entirely, then started the tricky job of getting off the ice on the front skis alone. By that time, the sun was gone. White-out had shut down completely. They could no longer see the old ski tracks. McIntyre lined his ship up as best he could, attempted a blind take-off and made it. He also made a difficult landing on the sea-ice airstrip at Kotzebue with visibility reduced to zero by thick, blowing snow. But he's the first to admit he was very, very lucky.

Polar-bear hunting may seem very much like a pastime invented by a handful of men who decided jai-alai or skin-diving for sharks was too tame. Actually, it's growing rapidly in popularity. This simple fact is quite a tribute to the courage of American hunters.

Until very recent years, ice-bear hunting as a sport was practically unknown. Most of the enormous white pelts that hung on library and livingroom walls a few decades back were either purchased from the coastal Eskimos or taken by whaling ships.

Before today's light planes with powerful engines were designed, polar-bear hunting was an extremely expensive and involved undertaking. The aircraft of that day were either too heavy to come down on the ice or else lacked the power to be considered safe for use in the Arctic. The range of the white bear is always the edge of the pack, never the more solid ice nearer the pole. He lives on the fringe of the cap, where bergs and pan-ice meet open stretches of water. Before World War II, polar-bear hunting meant working slowly through the floes in a small boat.

Even with modern methods, ice-bear hunting is still slightly more expensive than brownie or grizzly hunting. A charter plane usually costs forty or fifty dollars an hour. If this seems high, remember that good hunting conditions exists through less than three months of the year. Remember, in addition to white-out and unsafe ice, the flash blizzards and screaming gales that can come up abruptly and trap a small plane away from shore. Remember that, out of the twelve planes that hunted polar bears in Alaska last season, three were lost. Remember that planes are expensive and that the life-expectancy of a man in the water of the Arctic Ocean is less than three minutes.

No guide can honestly guarantee a white bear or even give an estimate of the flight time required. Polar bears have never really been plentiful. There are probably no more than 3,000 on the ice off the Alaskan coast today. In the twenty years previous to World War II, only 1,300 hides found their way into the fur markets of the world.

Polar bears are found all the way around the top of the globe. No one area has an abundance of them, but the greatest concentrations of them seem to be between Point Hope and Point

Barrow and east of Victoria Strait toward Greenland. There hunting grounds on the edge of the polar cap are forever shifting, and this makes solitary world travelers out of them. They wander far south in the winter, north again in the summer. They drift down through the Bering Strait or even float to the bottom of Hudson Bay. Often they chase the herds of seals down the coast of Labrador. Polar bears have even been known to enter the Gulf of St. Lawrence, just a few hundred miles north of Maine.

When the long Arctic night shuts down, their hunting range is increased greatly. Life becomes a desperate, frantic battle against starvation as they depend on their predatory skill to carry them through long months of unending darkness and cold and hunger. Polar-bear hunting in mid-winter would be nothing more than a quick but unpleasant method of committing suicide.

The only production rifles really suitable for use on polar bears are the .300 and .375 H. & H. Magnums. Custom weapons like the .300 Weatherby Magnum are even better. It's true that bears have been killed with much smaller rifles. But it's also true that a case is on record of an ice bear covering more than 60 yards in a charge after being shot through the heart several times with 180-grain 30-06 slugs. A wounded polar bear is a deadly, savage antagonist. In the terrible, fearsome rush he makes to destroy an enemy, he reaches a speed of 25 miles an hour. There are no trees to climb on the ice pack. Even when not wounded, a hungry white bear can see you a mile away and scent you even farther. His coloring makes him all but invisible during his silent, belly-flat stalk. The absurd notion that using a small-caliber rifle is more sporting is hardly worthy of mention. As in all other kinds of hunting, the most sporting weapon is one capable of killing instantly if used properly.

In addition to securing a proper rifle, the sportsman who wishes to hang the skin of a great white bear in his trophy room might lessen the top-heavy odds against him slightly by investigating the several types of insulated survival clothing that have recently appeared on the market. Some of these are designed to keep a man afloat as well as keep him from freezing. Although most Alaskan guides are sticking to their furs and mukluks over heavy layers of woolens, many of these new items of outdoor wear look extremely promising.

Polar-bear hunting time is from February through April, the months when the days have grown long enough to allow flying, the ice is at its best and hides are prime. Since the best time for the big Alaskan brownies is late April through early May, it's possible to make a single trip and hunt the two largest flesh-eating, four-legged animals in existence.

This two-trophy expedition could hardly be described as a workingman's special. But the expense will be considerably smaller than the cost of an African or Indian trip. The out-fitting company will be less commercial. On a lion or tiger hunt, the sportsman is usually expected to take the first shot offered him. Most Alaskan guides are very pleased to get a fighter who wants to try for the record books, no matter how many shots this means passing up.

The Boone and Crockett Club considers hide lengths to be unreliable and accepts only skull measurements. But the polar bear has an extremely small head in relation to his size. Until a portable scale capable of weighing a giant bear in the field is invented, hide lengths will continue to be the only basis of comparison between brown and white bears, reliable or not.

The best brownie hide on record was taken on Kodiak Island in 1930. It measured ten feet four inches in length. The biggest polar bear, killed sixteen years earlier, taped out an even twelve feet. That's a very long piece of fur. But with today's rapidly-increasing interest in ice-bear hunting, that 42-year-old record could fall at any time.

Within the forseeable future, it's doubtful that the polar bear could be threatened with extinction. The kind of sports-men who have the nerve and daring essential to ice-bear hunting are not the type of men who exterminate any species. The Point Hope Eskimos hunt them for food and for the twelve dollars per foot of length their hides bring in the market. But taking a dog team out onto the ice pack is a difficult and dangerous undertaking. This market hunting does not seriously affect the bears' numbers.

Destruction of habitat is always the main factor in driving a predator species down the one-way trail to oblivion. Until some commercial value is found in the pack-ice of the Arctic Ocean, the great white bear is relatively safe.

The sportsman who is seriously considering a polar-bear hunt should never allow hiself to be lulled into false confidence by the playful, clowning ice bears he sees across the moats or through the bars of big-city zoos. For some reason, probably because he's fed regularly, the polar bear takes very readily to captivity. Here, small children stare in delight at the antics of this large white beast with a black mouth that looks like a creature from another planet.

But up in his own untamed world, up where white-out fogs the air and blowing snow camouflages the treacherous new ice, he's a very different animal. He's 1500 or more pounds of white-furred fury, a beast with the strength of a half-dozen lions or tigers and the speed and ferocity of a black Muira bull. He's a creature designed by Nature to prey on all others and be preyed on by none. He's the great white bear of the Arctic ice pack, the undisputed King of the North. And he's far from willing to relinquish his reign to the puny, two-legged creature called Man.

He's the most dangerous big-game animal in the world.

The hunter who makes the two-trophy expedition mentioned earlier will discover that, after braving the anger of the Arctic Ocean, his quest for a big brown bear can be undertaken in as much comfort, luxury and style as he can afford. One guide at Kodiak uses a de luxe express cruiser, extremely modern lodges ashore with all conveniences, and caters to men who wish to bring their wives along. Many others boast such things as electricity and running water in their camps.

Of course, no degree of easy living will lessen in any way the excitement and danger of the moment when the hunter meets his brownie. Without any fear of exaggeration it can be said that the sight of a giant Kodiak bear rearing up on his hind legs will scare most men literally out of their wits. When a brownie stretches to leave his claw marks on tree trunks, his front paws may be a full fourteen feet above the ground. That's not far from two stories high, in terms of the modern home or apartment. The hunter who brings back a brown-bear hide must keep his nerve during the shock of this initial meeting, then place a shot well with a heavy rifle. As often as not, he must stand his ground and face a charge. This unbelievably huge creature fears nothing in this world, even automobiles and airplanes. His great jaws can snap a two-by-four like a match stick. It's an old saying in the Territory that the average big-game hunter gets his brownie with two shots—his and the guide's.

The most common method of hunting the brown bear is to climb to a good look-out point and keep watch on the surrounding countryside with binoculars. Once a trophy-sized bear is sighted, a slow and skillful stalk is the next move.

Hunting the inland silvertipped grizzly has a great deal in common with hunting his larger brown cousin. As a matter of fact, the dividing line between brownies and silvertips is far from clear and distinct. The best way to get a group of zoology professors to take off their glasses and start swinging at each other is to ask them how many species of bears exist in North America.

In the years when the opinions of Ernest Seton were regarded as law in the world of natural history, it was generally accepted that only three kinds of bears roamed this continent—the black bear, the grizzly and the polar bear. Both the brownies and the silvertips were regarded as grizzlies.

Shortly afterward, several scientists insisted that there was too much variation in the skulls of grizzlies to consider them a single species. When new attempts at classification were made, naturalists had a field day. Anyone with a college degree who saw a bear in the woods immediately proclaimed a new species, usually naming it after himself. One enthusiastic re-classifier ended up by cataloguing eighty-four species of grizzly, five of them on one small island alone. Although grizzlies were growing scarce, facing extinction over most of their former range, Latin names were flourishing and multiplying like rabbits.

Today, a good many naturalists have gone back to the classifications Seton made and insist that a single but highly variable species of grizzly is found on this continent. For record-book purposes, the Boone and Crockett Club attempts to erase the confusion by listing all bears killed in certain coastal regions as brownies and all other grizzlies as silvertips. This is necessary because the hides of grizzlies may vary in color from blackish-gray through all shades of brown and buff to nearly white. Pale, faded grizzlies in extreme northern Canada and Alaska are often mistaken for polar bears.

The maximum weight of silvertips today, now that the giant California grizzly is extinct, is probably slightly over 1100 pounds. The heaviest brownie on record weighed out at 1656 pounds. Such a bear would have a skull eighteen or nineteen inches in length. Its neck would be five feet in circumference. Its hind feet would be eighteen inches long; its front ones, a foot wide.

From the hot mountains of Sonora to the barren tundra north of the Brooks Range, the habits of North American grizzlies are remarkably similar. Both the bears of the near-tropics and the bears of the Arctic seem to mate in June or July and give birth to their cubs in January or February. A sow usually has only one cub at her first whelping. After that, she has twins, triplets, or very rarely litters of four.

Father grizzlies, like all other bears, assume no responsibility for their young. In fact, a boar bear will readily kill and eat his own cubs if he finds them unprotected. But this seldom occurs. A mother bear is always doting and extremely watchful. Any wild creature that annoys her offspring is usually committing suicide.

Hibernation periods vary according to climate. In the coldest sections of bear country, the bruins may disappear in October and not come out again until early May. In the southern United

States a bear usually goes into his winter sleep for no more than a few days at a time. Like polar bears, the grizzlies of the Far North hole up in the caverns formed by buckled ice. Temperate-zone bears choose a cave, a rockpile, a hollow tree or log, or even merely a dense thicket. A hibernating bear is merely sleeping, not spending the winter in some sort of frozen trance as is so often believed. His body temperature is normal. His rate of breathing is about the same as a sleeping human. Sometimes he is semi-conscious. At other times he is wide awake and perfectly capable of defending himself against any intruder.

A grizzly rules his range, which may be thirty to seventy miles across, and fears no enemies except man. The strength of these bears is literally beyond belief. A brownie once dragged her three-quarter-ton dead mate a hundred yards up a near-vertical cliff. Silvertips have been seen walking off effortlessly with the carcasses of giant bull elk, moose and even bison.

It's part of American folklore that the vitality of the grizzly is close to supernatural, that these giants have charged and killed hunters with their hearts shot out or their brains blown away. Modern naturalists have disputed this and insisted that a grizzly has less tenacity of life than a mountain goat, for example. Perhaps it's only natural for a hunter to be more impressed with a creature that runs toward him with a bullet in its heart than with one that runs away. At any rate, there can be little doubt that a wounded grizzly seems very determined to stay alive long enough to avenge himself. Two hunters were once pursued for a full half-mile by a silvertip with a broken spine. When this bear finally gave in to death, the fur was completely worn from its dragging hind legs.

Freedom from natural enemies makes these creatures comparatively long-lived, but it's extremely doubtful that any bear reaches an age greater than forty years. It has been claimed that seventy-year-old musket balls have been found in the flesh of brownies killed recently. But it must be remembered that the Russian seal and salmon poachers of only a few decades ago often carried antiquated weapons. Bears in the protection of zoological parks have rarely lived beyond thirty.

Most bruins are extremely playful creatures when left undisturbed. Grizzlies are far more dignified than black bears but even the gigantic brownies have been seen sliding down the snow-covered slopes like otters on their heavy-furred rumps, then climbing up to slide again.

Within the forty-eight states, the question of whether the grizzly should be granted strict protection as a valuable game animal or should be treated as a livestock-killing outlaw is strictly academic. With the exception of a few near-tame animals in national parks and a few more in captivity, there are almost none left to protect. Although a few survivors still exist in several scattered stretches of cover, Alaska and British Columbia are the only remaining areas with a large enough grizzly population to interest the trophy hunter.

The battle of extermination fought against the grizzly in the Western United States was second in bitterness and intensity only to the war waged on the gray wolf. Very little of this slaughter was deserved. A cattle-raiding grizzly was always a rarity. But this mighty and impressive creature is gone from the plains and the Rockies and no power on earth is going to bring him back.

We should be able to examine the grizzly's rapid plunge to extinction in the West and learn a few lessons that would insure his permanent survival in Alaska. But even here we are failing miserably. Brownies and silvertips alike, harassed unmercifully by hostile cattle-raising, salmon-fishing and lumbering interests, have been making an uphill fight for survival ever since the Territory's population first began booming. Chances are that good grizzly hunting would exist nowhere south of the Brooks Range if it had not been for the constant efforts of a number of conservationists here in the States who have devoted themselves tirelessly to the cause of the giant bears.

On his Canadian range, the grizzly is faring considerably better. The highest concentration of silvertips found anywhere in the world is in the coastal mountains of British Columbia. The Canadian government seems to have finally recognized just how valuable an asset the big bear is and how carefully he should be conserved.

A good many American hunters, however, will never be able to afford a trip to the range of the silvertip or the brownie, much less a charter flight over the fringe of the polar cap. For them, big-game hunting consists of trips to close-to-home forests after whitetail deer. These same forests are usually also the home of the black bear, considerably smaller than the giants of the north but still a trophy most hunters prize even above a many-pointed rack of deer horns. Yet, in spite of the fact that blackie country exists within a day's drive of nearly every city in this country, very few men deliberately hunt bear.

A number of bruins are killed by deer hunters each fall, usually roused from hibernation by a sudden thaw and then crowded into the range of someone's rifle by the sheer pressure of the number of men in the forest. But these are accidental deaths. The resulting trophy is certainly no testimonial to the skill and knowledge of the man who hangs it on his wall.

The black bear has adapted himself and learned to live close to man. In doing so his senses have been sharpened and his wariness increased until his ability to keep himself out of sight is nothing short of miraculous. For this reason, a pack of large well-trained hounds has become a necessity in modern bear hunting unless the area hunted has an unusually numerous bear population or unless spring hunting is allowed.

There are men who own such dogs in the vicinity of nearly every stretch of bear country. Some of them stage organized hunts frequently and invite the public. Practically all of them are willing and eager to make up a small portion of the cost of dog food by the half-ton lot and hire themselves out to men who are seriously interested in shooting a bear. A letter to the conservation department of your state will put you in touch with such houndsmen. You'll be surprised at how little they charge in comparison with professional guides.

In states where spring hunting is allowed and bears are plentiful, dogs are hardly needed. For a few weeks after coming out of hibernation the black bear seems to be less cautious than usual and ventures out of the thick cover a good deal. In mountainous country, keeping watch with binoculars and then stalking is the best method. In our eastern and northern forests, sitting still and waiting at a likely spot is the most certain way of bringing home a bear hide.

The best advice that can be given to hunters who do not live in the vicinity of Maine or California and wish to make a bear-hunting trip with a better than even chance of success is to try Ontario.

Back in the mid-Twenties the bottom dropped out of the market for blackie hides and Ontario trappers hung up their bear traps. As a result, this province has a black-bear population that is matched only by a few Alaskan areas. Very little hunting was done during World War II and in the years immediately afterward the number of blackies increased to a level that was out of all proportion to the deer and moose herds. Rather than resort to antiquated methods of control like bounties or hired government hunters, Ontario very sensibly decided to combine bear control with increasing its tourist business by opening a special spring season and offering a non-resident license at a low token price.

The rates at Ontario lodges and camps compare favorably with those in the States. Ontario guides get ten dollars a day, considerably less than the thirty-five an Alaskan guide costs you. In some sections, guides are required by law. But there are a good many stretches of bear country where a hunter with reasonable ability to take care of himself in the woods can save the expense of a guide.

My own personal favorite area lies on either side of the Chapleau Road, some distance north of Thessalon. I defy any hunter who is merely capable of sitting still and keeping quiet to camp for a few days in this forest and not get a shot at a blackie.

A good many of us Michigan hunters have our own way of going after Ontario bears. We make use of the lumber camps.

At about the same time the blackies come out of hibernation the jacks leave the camps and the white-water men begin the drive downriver. The deserted camps contain bunks and mattresses, firewood and even food. The hunter who does not abuse the privilege is welcome. In effect, he has a free hunting lodge.

These camps attract bears like a magnet. In addition to the garbage pits there are usually a few dead horses about to tease a blackie's sensitive nostrils.

Last spring I parked my car near the mouth of the Rapid River at about sundown one evening and hiked three miles up through the hills to a camp. Bear tracks were everywhere. Bears had raided the mess hall and scattered the big hard loaves of bread all about the area. I caught a couple of hours sleep, then started keeping watch. The blackies waited until just after the moon went down to show up. I saw one full-grown bear who spooked before I could size him up, then a young two-year-old I didn't want, finally a big male. The first shot snapped his spine, but going into the spruces to finish him off by flashlight was a little tricky. Most of the men who insist that bear hunting at night is unsporting have never tried it. I waited until dawn to skin him out, then packed the hide back down to the car. The rest of the time I'd allowed for my spring bear-hunting trip was spent fishing.

This was not a rare or unusual experience. It was a rather typical night of Ontario bear hunting. There are very few places left on the North American continent where such hunting is possible. Although it seems strange that a creature who has adapted himself to the pressure of civilization as well as the black bear has should ever be threatened with extinction, the fact is that the future of the blackie is becoming increasingly clouded. A new law has just been passed in California that legalizes the poisoning of bears. The conservation departments of many other states have recently extended their seasons and liberalized the allowable methods of hunting. Our Michigan bear population has dwindled alarmingly in the last few years. The black bear's habitat has been threatened in every session of Congress, as special-interest groups seek control of our national forests.

There is no sensible reason whatsoever why the black bear should not be a permanent part of this nation's wildlife. Unlike the grizzly, this bear has the ability to prosper in areas that are relatively close to civilization. There is no excuse for forcing his numbers down to a level that would destroy bear-hunting as a sport and recreation.

There is little danger that sportsmen will ever drive the black bear or any other creature over the brink of extinction. Only the exterminators can do that, either by direct slaughter or by eliminating the forestland from the surface of this country.

XI

BEARS THAT HUNT MEN

If you take a vacationtime motoring trip through Michigan's Upper Peninsula you'll doubtlessly spend a day at Sault Ste. Marie, site of the famed Soo Locks. Your next stop will probably be the beautiful Tahquamenon Falls and you'll drive west on Highway 28.

You'll notice a scarcity of towns on this concrete thread through the wilderness. A little gravel road branching off to your right leads to Brimley. Farther on, you'll pass through Raco.

On your left is the Marquette National Forest, an expanse of land on which the only marks of men are a few dirt-rut roads and the high pointed fire towers that look vaguely like oil derricks, each with a neat little cabin near its base.

The afternoon of July 7, 1948, was a typical day of Michigan's short hot summer. The back door of the fire-tower cabin at Mission Hill, the home of Arthur Pomranky and his family, had been left open, but the screen had been closed tightly to keep flies from the kitchen. Pomranky was at work. A neighbor woman was visiting his wife. Both the children were playing. Allan was in the basement below. Little three-year-old Carol Ann was in the backyard close to the porch.

The forest is peaceful in summer. And the cabin at Mission Hill was almost a part of the forest, set in a small clearing, ringed tightly by dense thickets of second-growth hardwood—

just as though the wilderness was silently trying to choke out any further advance of civilization. But with unbelievable suddenness, the drowsy quiet was shattered by a child's terrified scream. The afternoon became a nightmare in bright daylight.

Mrs. Pomranky jumped from her chair and ran to the door. Carol Ann was on her knees on the porch, one hand grasping for the screen, shrieking steadily. A black bear was halfway up the steps when the horrified mother first saw it. But this creature looked nothing like the comical, begging bruins that amuse the tourists in roadside zoos.

This bear was thin and lean. Its eyes burned with viciousness and determination. Its jaws parted with a snarl, baring massive fangs. All at once it lunged on up, snatched the screaming baby girl in its jaws and threw her from the porch to the ground. It turned and pounced on her, roaring its defiance at the doorway once more, then picking her up by the arm.

With no thought for her own life, Mrs. Pomranky started after the child. But as the bear turned and charged back up the steps, the other woman grabbed the frantic mother, pulled her back into the kitchen and slammed the door.

The only weapon in the Mission Hill cabin was a 32-20 Colt revolver. Nearly insane with desperation, Mrs. Pomranky ran to find it. Her hands were shaking so badly that loading it seemed an endless, impossible task. She gave up and, unarmed, ran out through the door into the backyard.

The clearing was empty. There was no further screaming, no sound of movement in the brush. The quiet of a summer afternoon had surged back.

Mrs. Pomranky fought off hysteria just long enough to get to the telephone and dial the Ranger Station at Raco.

Ranger Bruce Elliott heard the story, hung up the phone and went into action. Nothing in the manual covered this situation. A renegade bear is a monstrous rarity. Hunting one down and destroying it quickly requires not only skilled hunters but experienced dogs. The nearest man with a pack of specially-trained bearhounds was Carl Johnson, who lived in the Lower Peninsula, more than 150 miles away.

The best local hunter was Alex Van Luven, a former state trapper who was then employed at the Ellis Wilcox Mill at Iriquoid Point. Ranger Elliott got word of the tragedy out to the mill, then snatched his rifle from its rack and hurried toward Mission Hill.

At about ten minutes after three, Alex Van Luven and seven fellow workers learned of the attack on the Pomranky home. Dropping their work instantly, the mill crew started south. Alex left the others and sped over to his home in Brimley to pick up his dog, a three-year-old Labrador retriever. Racing over twisting, narrow dirt roads again, he drove on toward the fire tower, clearly visible above the forest in the distance.

A large group of searchers was waiting for him. Three men from the Ranger Station had already gone into the brush, but Deputy Sheriff Randolph Wilson had ordered the rest to wait until Alex arrived with the dog. No one had any idea what direction the raider bear had taken.

Alex Van Luven assumed immediate charge of the hunt. He chose four men from the group and told them to follow him but stay behind the dog and leave the track unfouled. He asked Wilson to keep the rest of the men out of the woods until he sent word back. Looking over all sides of the clearing he picked the cover to the west for the first attempt.

He moved through the thickness slowly and let the dog test every bit of the cover ahead. They had gone perhaps a hundred yards into the forest when the fur on the Labrador's back sprang up and he strained at his leash, his muzzle pressed tight to the leaves. Just then Alex heard a shout from one of the rangers who had started out before him.

With the others close behind, he hurried on, smashing his way through the tight growth. He found the ranger kneeling beside a series of scuff-marks in the leaves. One of Carol Ann's shoes lay nearby. Splotches of blood marked the ground.

After fifty yards of steady trailing, the Labrador led them to what was left of Carol Ann Pomranky.

The three-year-old girl had died with both eyes open and her lips widely parted. She lay on her back, her head propped up by the trunk of a small oak sapling. Her clothing hung loosely from her body, most of it untorn. The killer bear had merely pushed it aside as it fed. The child's abdomen, stomach and thighs were gone. Her left calf had also been eaten. A length of intestine was draped across a nearby bush. Carol Ann's neck and head were deeply gashed. One fang mark on the left temple looked as though it had reached the brain. The men who stared in horror at that butchered body could only hope that this death blow had been dealt early.

Strangely enough, the baby's face was unmarked. Indescribable terror and agony were permanently frozen in those features.

The men in that hunting party were all tough and hardened woodsmen. But none of them wanted to take a second look at Carol Ann.

Alex Van Luven asked for a volunteer to stay with the body. He realized there was only a remote chance the bear would return to its kill. Most likely, it was bolting off to the west, frantic to put a wide stretch of forest between itself and the disturbance it had caused. But Alex also knew that this was no ordinary bear. It had already broken every conceivable rule of behavior. There could be no predicting its actions. A man named Wayne Weston offered to keep watch at the spot.

Next, Alex sent two men back to the Mission Hill tower to give orders to the waiting hunters. He wanted them to hurry around and spread out along a road the bear would have to cross if it kept on to the west. With only one man left beside him, he unsnapped the leash from his dog.

The Labrador trailed steadily and surely for another fifty yards, then lost the scent. With a sudden suspicion that the bear had doubled back here, Alex set his dog to casting out the loss, working in increasing circles.

All at once, something moved in the brush behind them.

Alex whirled and snapped the safety on his rifle. But the new-comer was only a German shepherd dog. It belonged to the man who had remained with them. It had trailed them from the clearing.

The German shepherd distracted the hard-working Labrador so much that Alex told its owner to take it on ahead.

After a few more minutes of wide casting, the Labrador recovered the line and started north, trailing rapidly. The track was very fresh and it became impossible to keep the unleashed dog in sight. Alex was far too busy dodging and breaking his way through the thick, tangled cover to worry about the fact that he was now hunting alone.

The chase led directly up the side of a steep ridge. By the time the hunter got to the top, his dog had gone on out of hearing. Alex kept moving to the northwest, guessing at direction.

Suddenly he stopped short, knelt and examined the ground. The earth was just soft enough to show the wide impression of a bear track.

It led directly back toward the spot where Carol Ann's body had been found.

Wayne Weston had been waiting in silence for some time. The sounds of voices and movement through the brush had faded and died. The hunt had gone on without him. He was left out of it. His eyes still regularly searched the surrounding cover. But he was standing his watch without hope.

All at once, he looked across a short stretch of forest and saw the bear. There had been no noise, no apparent movement. The creature seemed to have just suddenly materialized in the thicket beyond the oak with the little mangled figure at its base. The shaggy killer had returned to feed.

Weston's first bullet deflected itself on the bushes that screened the bear. In the split second that it took to rack up another cartridge he could see the animal hesitate, then come on. His second and third shots drove directly into the bear's chest and it stumbled and fell, snapping and kicking convulsively. Two more shots and the thrashing stopped.

The man-hunter of Mission Hill was dead.

The killer-bear was a full-grown animal and yet it weighed out at a mere 125 pounds. Conservation Department officials took the carcass into Sault Ste. Marie. The county coroner called a local veterinarian into consultation. A careful, scientific examination identified the animal beyond any possible doubt. Its stomach was opened up. Three pounds and ten ounces of human flesh were found. The stomach contained nothing else except a few ants and a little grass. The carcass was then frozen and flown down to the Conservation Department laboratories at Lansing.

Like a wilderness fire, the story of the attack on the Pomranky girl spread to the little northwoods towns that surround the forest long before it went out on the A.P. wire to be converted into columns of newsprint. We who gave no thought to the bear tracks we saw in the woods, we who often drove our children over to the township dumps on spring evenings in hopes of giving them a glimpse of a bear, listened in shocked disbelief. Why? Why had this happened? What caused an ordinary harmless bear to turn killer?

Theories and rumors followed fast. We first heard that the killer bear had gotten mixed up with a porcupine, that the infection and pain of quills in its jaws had driven it mad. The next explanation was that this bear had been suffering from a previous bullet wound and bore a deep grudge against mankind. Then the story went out that this was an escaped tame bear, unable to find food in the wild, unafraid of men. Some of these fanciful guesses were dignified on the front pages of newspapers, as the big-circulation dailies of the cities to the south sought to give their subscribers the explanation they demanded. None of these rumors came from the laboratories in Lansing. And none of them was true.

Microscopic examinations were made of the creature's brain and spinal cord but nothing unusual was found. There was no evidence of rabies. There were no marks on the hide, no worn-off fur to indicate that the animal had ever been held in captivity. There were no old wounds. The only way in which the renegade bear of Mission Hill differed from a normal wild bear was its extremely starved condition. Not an ounce of fat was found in its body.

The best experts available were allowed to make detailed examinations and test their theories. But they were all forced to accept the obvious. Only one conclusion was possible.

For the first time in the entire history of this country, a bear had attacked, killed and eaten a human being, motivated only by hunger.

And this unheard-of assault had been committed not by the ferocious silvertip, not by the gigantic brownie, but by an animal universally regarded by naturalists as absolutely inoffensive.

The common black bear has long been underrated in every way from his size to his ferocity. I've known of two different black bears that scaled out at well over 600 pounds, taken by Michigan archers in recent years. I have yet to see a wildlife text that admits these bruins reach anything near this size. The myth that the blackie is perfectly harmless seems to dominate nearly everything written about him. In reality, the same provocation that brings a grizzly or brownie to attack man will also make a killer out of their smaller relative. It's true that the black bear is less aggressive when hunted, less likely to charge when wounded. But he's also less cautious. And in protected areas and refuges he loses his fear of man far more readily.

Black bears like the man-hunter of Mission Hill are fantastically rare. Beyond any doubt, their mental make-up is abnormal. But they *do* exist. They violate every rule of wildlife behavior that naturalists can determine. They make wildlife study both fascinating and exasperating. For no matter what the species, there seems to be as much individual variation among wild creatures as among men. Nothing is more ridiculous than expecting all animals to act in the same way when faced with the same situation.

160

Strangely enough, the savagery of the grizzly bear is usually over-rated. Contrary to pioneer legend and folklore, the big silvertips rarely hunt down men, very seldom attack without good reason. Most often, when you meet one of these shaggy, solitary giants in the wild, he's interested only in avoiding you and lumbers hurriedly away. Occasionally, an unusually brave one will merely go on along his way and expect you to do the same.

The famous predator-hunter, Ben Lilly, once wrote that a grizzly under two years of age will fight only for freedom, even when wounded. A sow grizzly from three to six years old will also attack to defend her young, but a male of that age still fights only to escape. However, once a silvertip is six or more years old he may attack anything or anyone he has reason to believe is an enemy. This sounds extremely logical. Even in cases of unprovoked attack, the bear was usually given some justification for thinking himself in danger.

Grizzlies and black bears alike are more vegetarian than meat-eater. But the greater strength, speed and intelligence of the big silvertips enable them to prey more successfully on deer and elk herds and even raid livestock. A few grizzlies have been notorious cattle killers.

Probably the most famous bear of American history was Old Mose, a silvertip that survived 35 years of intensive hunting by the cattlemen near the Black Mountains of Colorado. Raiding over a 75-mile domain, this clever grizzly avoided mine-fields of poison and steel traps. He seemed to have a personal grudge, an understandable one, against the advance of civilization. There was no mistaking his track. Whenever broken fences or slaughtered livestock were found, two missing toes correctly identified the big outlaw. In his lifetime, Old Mose killed five men, butchered 800 head of cattle and did an estimated 30,000 dollars' damage. In April of 1904, he was finally cornered by the hound pack of a hunter. It took eight shots to kill him.

Old Mose was a rare animal. Few grizzlies are destructive to livestock. Even fewer are dangerous to man. Raider-bears and killer-bears alike are exceptions, always.

The silvertip has invariably been considered the most ferocious of bears, even by the scientists who named him *ursus horribilis*. But in modern times attacks on men have come most often from his salmon-eating relatives, the brown bears. Brownies kill a man every couple of years in Alaska and badly maul many others.

Although the brown bear is merely another race of grizzly, he differs from the inland bears in more ways than one. A killer-silvertip often assaults a man with smashing blows from his forepaws. In every case where a human being was mauled by a brownie, the bear's jaws alone were used. The brown bear's most effective weapons are his claws—four or five inches long, pointed and sharp and backed by a mountain of muscle. But in battle he seems to use them only to pull his enemy within reach of his teeth.

Just a few years ago, a trapper named King Thurman left his cabin in the lonely expanse of Alaska's Chickaloon Flats region. He was going for water and he carried only a bucket. He considered a rifle an unnecessary bit of weight on so short a trip. When he was little more than a hundred yards from his home, a bear jumped him, mauled him horribly and left him for dead. The reason for this attack will never be known. Many things about this incident will never be known. Tracks, blood stains and a few painfully scribbled words were the only record.

When Thurman regained consciousness his first feeling was most likely a vague surprise at still being alive. Shock must have been dulling the pain at that moment, because the will to go on living was strong enough to start him crawling back, inch by inch, toward his cabin. The jaws of the bear had torn his right side completely apart from his shoulder to his calf, torn his ribs loose from his backbone. His left hip and right arm were also severely mauled. Only the length of a football field lay between him and his shack, but the distance must have seemed infinitely great as he painted the pathway bright with his blood.

162

When this ordeal was over and he lay on the floor of his cabin, King Thurman first realized the hopelessness of his situation. Had he realized it sooner, he would never have forced himself on along that pathway. He had no neighbors and expected no visitors. He'd lived a life of loneliness. Now a lonely death awaited him. He took a pencil in his left hand. His right had been too thoroughly chewed up to hold one. He pulled the form of an old claim notice in front of him.

HAVE BEN TORE UP BY A BROWN BEAR NO SHOW TO GET OUT GOOD BY

Printed in wobbly, near-illegible letters, the words ran down the page in a single column, one above the other, very much like a schoolchild's spelling paper.

With his life draining out onto the rough cabin floor, King Thurman waited for some time before making another attempt at writing. Most likely it was then, with the numbing effect of shock wearing off, that he first felt the full pain of the terrible damage done to his body.

SANE BUT SUFFERING was all that could be deciphered on his second message. Several words followed but no one could read them.

His agony increased. The pain became unbearable. Whether or not he had reached his decision by the time he made his third try at writing cannot be determined. Two illegible words obscure the meaning of his tortured thought.

THE ——— ——— OF DEATH

Technically, King Thurman wasn't killed by the brownie. When he was found, his rifle lay on the floor beside him, powder burns and a small swollen hole marked his forehead and the back of his skull was blown off.

Will a bear make an unprovoked attack on a human being?

The death of Carol Ann Pomranky should settle this question once and for all. Certainly the child did nothing to harm or infuriate the bear. But this is a point that has been hotly debated by naturalists for years. Chances are that the iron-clad case of the Mission Hill killer will be ignored and the debate will continue.

Perhaps the answer rests entirely upon the meaning of the word unprovoked.

In one sense, no attack takes place without provocation. Charging or springing upon men, mauling or killing them, is abnormal behavior for a bear. No wild creature breaks the habits of a lifetime without reason. But there have been a few cases where the outlaw bear kept his reasons strictly to himself and men could only guess at what made a killer out of him.

In fully 95 percent of all bear-attack cases, the assault is definitely provoked. A hunter seriously wounds a bear. In rage and pain, the creature turns on him.

In the late morning of October 20, 1956, 29-year-old Ken Scott and 45-year-old Viv Squires, both of Fort Benton, Montana, followed the track of an elk into a thickly-wooded ravine high in the mountains of the Bob Marshall Wilderness Area. They spread out in working their way through the dense cover, half-expecting a big trophy bull to be flushed out onto the slope above.

All at once, the ravine came to life. Squires heard something big coming his way. He dodged ahead and tried to find an opening for a shot. But it was no elk that had been flushed from cover. Viv Squires suddenly found himself face to face with a grizzly.

He tried to jump to one side, but the brush caught his feet and he fell. Instantly the bear was on top of him. Squires kicked out frantically to keep the massive tusk-like fangs away. The grizzly's teeth ripped easily through the leather boots.

The giant bear, at this time, was not hunting or attacking men, but merely trying to escape. Satisfied that the hunter on the ground could not harm him now, he turned and bolted off in the opposite direction. Viv Squires pushed back to his feet.

"Grizzly!" he shouted at the top of his lungs. "He's coming your way, Kenny!"

Young Ken Scott was waiting at the top of a slight rise

when he heard his companion's yells and the crashing and snapping of branches as the grizzly charged toward him. He shot
once at moving brush. When he could finally see the bear he
took steady aim and he knew his second shot went home. But
the big silvertip merely turned aside and raced on out of sight.
Even though wounded now, he was still trying only to escape.

Scott was eager to begin following the blood trail that led
down off the ridge. He knew the 30-06 he carried was a capable-
enough grizzly rifle if handled by an expert shot. Scott knew
how to hunt and he knew how to shoot. Viv Squires wasn't so
eager. This was his first hunting trip in many years. He was no
marksman and the 30-30 he carried was strictly a deer rifle. But
when Scott pointed out they had no right leaving a wounded
grizzly to endanger other hunters, Squires gave in and they
began tracking together.

By mid-afternoon they'd entered a tight dark region of jack-
pines and second growth. They were tracking very slowly now.
The blood trail had thinned out and they could see only a few
yards ahead.

Ken Scott saw the grizzly first, still moving away from them.
Both men started shooting. Suddenly Scott's rifle jammed. He
yelled to Squires to keep firing and tried desperately to free the
action while his companion emptied all seven shots into the
wounded bear. All at once Ken saw the grizzly wheel about in its
tracks and come charging back. He shouted a warning. Viv Squires
jumped over a small embankment and ran on down the slope.
Scott saw the bear dodge to the side and start after Squires, so
he kept after his rifle action, prying at the jammed cartridge
with his jack-knife. He didn't see the grizzly turn back again.
He was still kneeling when the bear hit him.

Ken was pinned down tightly by long claws with almost a
half-ton of weight behind them. He felt his ribs being cracked,
but he couldn't move. Four different times he felt those great
jaws close on his head, ripping the flesh from his skull. As a
final defiant gesture the badly-wounded grizzly turned on its
back and rolled over the helpless man again and again.

Viv Squires thought Scott was just behind him as he raced away. Suddenly his mangled ankle went out from under him. He rolled on down the slope. When he could finally stop himself and get back to his feet, bruised and torn by the brush, he'd lost his rifle. It was then that he heard the roaring and screaming up in the jack-pines above him and realized the grizzly had caught Ken Scott.

As badly as he wanted to climb back and try to help, Squires knew better. Going back without a rifle would have done his friend no good. Going back would have meant only a futile waste of his own life. Forcing movement over the pain in his leg, trying to close his ears against the sounds of the battle above him, he started back at a run toward the spot where they'd left their horses early that morning.

Viv Squires ran a full mile, raced his horse for two more to reach camp. He found three other hunters there and they galloped back together. When they reached the spot where the bear had turned at bay, they found Ken Scott still alive and wide awake, still rational enough to remember every detail of his horrible ordeal. He was bleeding badly and most of the flesh and skin of his face and head hung in shreds from his skull. They carried him down the mountainside to a little creek and washed his wounds. There they built a fire and began discussing the problem of getting help. Squires would stay with Scott, they decided. The others would go after a first aid kit and start trying to get word out that a doctor was badly needed.

Suddenly one of the men heard something in the shadowy growth behind them. He looked around, then jumped to his feet shouting. The pain-crazed grizzly had returned in rage, determined to hunt down and punish the men who had hurt him. His entire hide seemed to be soaked with red. Blood was running steadily from his mouth.

The giant bear was only 20 feet away when a young hunter named Maurice Embleton stopped him with a well-placed neck shot from a .300 Savage. The grizzly collapsed and lay writhing until the hunters finished him off.

166

Practically everyone who was in the nearby mountains gave up elk hunting that day and joined in the battle for Ken Scott's life. Telephone lines were down and two men had to ride hard over 16 miles to Benchmark to send for help. Early the next morning a bush pilot landed nearby with a doctor from Great Falls. But Ken Scott died just an hour before help arrived. Whether medical care could have saved him or not is extremely doubtful. Considering the mauling he'd received, it's surprising that he lived through the night.

The death of Ken Scott illustrates well the general pattern that is evident in the very great majority of bear-attack cases. In no sense whatsoever could such an attack be considered unprovoked. A wounded bear is dangerous. And he has a right to be dangerous.

One little-known aspect of bear hunting is that the presence of a wounded bear can sometimes make man-killers out of other, unwounded bears. On several different occasions a hunter has followed the blood trail of a bear he's shot and then been jumped and killed by a completely different bear. This is a type of attack that is usually listed as unprovoked.

Only one out of twenty killer bears is anything other than a wounded, persecuted animal defending itself. But even in these rare cases some provocation can usually be found. Most of the time the bear was surprised and badly frightened. This is particularly true of female bears with cubs. The person who was attacked in this manner was usually moving through the cover with extreme quiet. Enough noise on his part to advertise his presence and lack of evil intentions would have saved his life.

Some years ago two miners were passing through a heavily-timbered region in Colorado. Neither of them was armed. They could see only a short distance in the thickness and they came very suddenly upon a mother grizzly with three cubs. The female bear struck only one quick defensive blow before hustling her whelps out of sight, but that blow crushed the skull of one man. The other was untouched.

Another main cause of so-called unprovoked attacks is the natural instinct of an unarmed man, upon meeting a bear face to face, to turn and run, and the natural instinct of a bear to chase and pounce upon anything that flees from it. These attacks could often be prevented. If a person meeting a bear merely stands still, the chances of the animal's doing anything more than turning and leaving are slight. In the rare cases where the bear continues to advance, stepping slowly aside, giving him the path and making no sudden movements will usually prevent an attack.

Ordinarily, when a wounded bear escapes a hunter, his natural fear of man is only deepened, his pain increases his caution and dread. But a few unusual bears have stalked, attacked and killed men because they were suffering from previously-incurred wounds. Sometimes these bears are in pain because of brushes with other wild creatures. More often they have been hurt by men.

In April of 1955 an Alaskan named Lloyd Pennington spotted a giant trophy grizzly while flying his small plane over the region just to the south of Mt. McKinley. Pennington circled a few times, following the patterns of mud-stained tracks until he'd located the silvertip's den. Then he winged his way back toward the nearest bit of civilization.

Spotting any bear except the polar bear from an airplane is supposed to be illegal. But since searching for campsites by air is allowed, the practice is widespread and impossible to prevent. Pennington had a friend in Anchorage named Everett Kendall who wanted a grizzly badly. Kendall arrived on April 16 and the two men took off on what promised to be a simple and successful bear hunt, a type of hunt that may soon force the Alaska Game Commission to outlaw all spring hunting.

Neither of the two men was ever seen alive again.

An air search finally located their bodies, lying in reddened snow on the very doorstep of the grizzly's den. When all of the tracks and bloodstains had been examined, a general account of

168

what had happened could be pieced together, although there is still some dispute about certain phases of the incident.

Pennington most likely located the den, then scouted the region from the air for some sign of the bear. He finally decided that the grizzly was in its den and landed at the nearest lake. Strapping on snowshoes, he and Kendall started up through the hills.

Very probably, as they walked across the rapidly-melting snow, both men were marveling at what an easy thing hunting the American King of Beasts has become when airplanes are used in earliest spring. Instead of packing into the wilderness area with horses and mules, spending several weeks sitting on a mountainside with binoculars and then making a long difficult stalk, an entire northern safari might well take no more than two hours.

The grizzly had trampled the snow around his den down hard and Pennington and Kendall removed their snowshoes before going closer. Kendall carried a powerful .300 Magnum and it's doubtful that he had any worries about the coming encounter. A few yards away from the opening Pennington motioned to Kendall to wait and to keep his rifle sights trained on the den mouth. Then he slipped around uphill on the left side of the den, listening carefully and staring into the shadows. After a long time he shook his head and started back down.

"He's not in there," he shouted.

Suddenly a small clump of scrub spruce on the far side of the den seemed to explode. The huge grizzly came to life abruptly out of cover that looked too sparse to conceal a small cub. He was onto Lloyd Pennington before he could lift his rifle, killing him instantly and racing on toward the other man.

Everett Kendall managed to fire one quick point-blank shot but it burned harmlessly through the flesh of the bear's forepaw. In violent rage the grizzly smashed at the hunter's head. The long claws raked half the flesh from Kendall's face and blinded him.

Kendall fought back with desperate courage. He fired every

169

cartridge in his rifle at this infuriated beast he could not see. Then he struck out again and again with his fists, tearing them to shreds on gnashing fangs. But finally he slumped to the snow, helpless but still alive.

He lived on for several hours while the gigantic grizzly poured out his rage on his surroundings and his two victims. The great bear bit through the trunks of scrub trees three inches thick. He tore open a box of cartridges that had fallen from Pennington's pocket and scattered them in the snow. Then he returned to Kendall, lay down beside him and began gnawing on his side. This was the wound that finally brought death. By then, death was most likely welcome.

After the two bodies were recovered, four hunters in two airplanes set out on a determined search to finish off the killer bear. His trail was not too difficult to follow from the air. A little over 20 miles from the den they sighted him and swooped down to blast him repeatedly with buckshot. But the pellets seemed to have no effect on the shaggy giant. Finally the planes were landed and the hunters set out after the bear on foot. He charged when they got too close but he went down under a steady stream of well-placed shots.

The best explanation for the unusual amount of aggressiveness possessed by this particular grizzly lies in the fact that another hunter was killed the year before in very nearly the same spot. He too had been attempting a two-hour grizzly hunt. He'd wounded a bear with a long-range shot, then followed a blood trail on foot while his guide went back to the plane to keep watch from the air. The grizzly had charged and killed the hunter, then escaped. It seems highly possible that the same animal was involved in both of these attack cases. Pennington and Kendall were most likely hunting a previously-wounded bear.

(Incidentally, neither of the two cases mentioned above dispute in any way the fine record of the Alaska Guides Association. No hunter has ever been killed or even mauled while being guided by an Association member and the very great majority

170

of first-rate Alaskan guides are members. Pennington did not have a guide's license, which meant he could legally offer his services only to resident Alaskans.)

A very rare type of killer bear is the one that assaults a man because he's carrying food of some sort. The last man killed in Yellowstone Park was a teamster who camped for the night in the heart of bear country and then slipped a large package of bacon under his pillow for safe-keeping. As nearly as the Park authorities could determine, the man woke to find the shaggy giant standing directly over him, its jaws close to his face. The man struck out in terror. The surprised bear killed him and was then so shocked at what had occurred that it ran off leaving the bacon behind.

Such a bear is not a normal wild bear. The animals in Yellowstone Park have not only lost their fear of man due to lack of hunting pressure, they have also lost the desire to seek their own meals. Tourists have fed them too often, left too much garbage for them to find. Sometimes they beg for food. Sometimes they demand it quite forcibly. The rules against feeding the bears or leaving the garbage anywhere except in the bear-proof containers are constantly being violated. It may not be too dangerous to feed these bears, but it is extremely dangerous to stop feeding them. Most people would be very shocked to learn how recently it has been necessary, for the protection of unthinking tourists, to chain these bears to trees and whip them in hopes of instilling a fear of man in them once more. Also, for the safety of tourists, a few more of the older grizzlies in the Park are shot each year.

The rarest of all killer bears are the ones like the man-hunter of Mission Hill, bears that deliberately seek out and attack a human being because of extreme hunger. If any blackie, silvertip or brownie ever committed such an assault previous to the Carol Ann Pomranky case, something must have prevented it from feeding on its victim. I know of only one other instance where one of these bears fed on human flesh. This occurred in Alaska in 1916, when a brownie bit a few chunks from the body of a long-dead drowning victim. Bears eat worms and grubs with relish. They consider the six-months-decayed carcass of a winter-killed deer to be a rare delicacy. But even killer bears seldom regard man as being fit to eat.

In all North America, in the entire world for that matter, there is only one creature that can honestly be called a habitual man-hunter, a creature with whom stalking and killing men for food is a normal behavior pattern. And this is the polar bear. With all other mammals, tigers and leopards and lions included, the man-hunting individual is an exception, most often a rare one. Actually, however, very few men have been killed by polar bears, since very few men have ever been within hundreds of miles of their range.

Should all bears be destroyed because a few have killed men?

This suggestion has often been made. In fact, a politician once campaigned for Congress with bear extermination his only program. Practically every time a man is attacked by a bear, no matter what the circumstances, certain groups and individuals immediately launch a drive to have all bears placed on the undesirable predator list and hunted and trapped into extinction at public expense. A little investigation usually reveals that this loud agitation is not coming from worried parents but from special interests who have long been eyeing the national forests as potential pastures, mines or timber tracts.

Incidents like the tragedy of Mission Hill are of course frightening and terrible, almost unbelievable. But even more unbelievable is just how seldom they occur. The bear who takes the life of a child is far more of a rarity among his species than the perverted murderer who does the same thing is among men. A little girl is actually far safer in the wildest part of Michigan's Upper Peninsula than in the heart of any large city in this country.

XII

THE EXTERMINATORS

A LITTLE more than a quarter-century ago, an Alaskan Forest Service employee by the name of Thayer decided to go brown-bear hunting. He was armed with an old Newton 30-06 and some cheap government-issue ammunition.

He climbed a slight rise and then stopped suddenly. Up ahead, in the fringe of an alder thicket, he saw his first brownie. The big heavy-furred beast was wandering peacefully through the cover, biting and chewing mouthfuls of grass. Thayer felt a growing elation as he raised his rifle and lined up the sights.

He'd been told not to try brown-bear hunting without a qualified guide. He'd been told a 30-06 was no weapon for a novice to be using on game this size and that service ammunition was useless in any sort of hunting. But he'd shrugged off advice and he felt very sure of himself now. The unsuspecting creature in the brush ahead was big enough, all right. But it looked very much like a huge Teddy bear.

Thayer squeezed the trigger and the rifle blast shattered the forest stillness. The hard-point, 150-grain bullet ripped through the bear's flesh without expanding and caused a wound that was neither fatal nor even crippling, but doubtlessly painful. With a bawling roar of surprise and rage, the brownie reared up on its hind legs. Its great head swung back and forth. Its deep-set little eyes searched intently.

Thayer started to rack up another cartridge. Then his hands froze on his rifle. This animal looked nothing like a Teddy bear now.

173

An angry brown bear standing upright is a terrifying sight. Sick and numb with fear, Thayer stared at the massive jaws and the long, tusk-like fangs, ten feet up. The heavy forepaws with the long claws dangled limply against the mountainous chest.

The great bear located the thing that was hurting it, then lunged forward and charged. Thayer dropped his rifle, turned and ran.

He lived only a few seconds longer.

His death caused the chairman of the Alaska Game Commission to issue a statement that should have been self-evident.

People who are not familiar with the habits and character of the brown bears should never shoot at these creatures unless they are absolutely certain they have the nerve to stand up under the charge of a wounded animal.

Thayer wasn't the first man to get himself killed by a brownie. Nor was he the last. This attack was a near-duplicate of most others in that it was definitely provoked and could easily have been prevented. But it very possibly had the furthest-reaching implications of any animal-attack case in history.

Just as the assassination of an archduke once brought the majority of the nations of the earth into war, this incident triggered an explosive conflict, a battle that is still being fought. Shortly after the attack story broke in the newspapers, a petition signed by a number of livestock owners who claimed to be residents of Kodiak Island was handed to the Game Commission.

Its demands, in brief, were that all the big brown bears, the largest flesh-eating animals left in the world, be exterminated.

Before the turn of the present century, the brown bear that died of anything but old age was a rarity among his species. But when the fur hunters had cleaned up the last pockets of buffalo from the central plains and a ready market for robes still existed, the hide of a brownie was an inviting substitute. Conservation came into being much too late to help the buffalo, but an aroused public did wake up in time to save the brownie from the hide hunters. In 1925 the Alaska Game Laws were passed.

Then two new threats to the giant bears rose up. Kodiak Island, the piece of brownie country that gives the big bruin his popular name, fell under the covetous glance of the livestock industry. At the same time, on the far side of the Gulf of Alaska, lumbering interests began estimating, in terms of pulpwood prices, the value of Admiralty Island, a wilderness paradise that contained more bears per square mile than any other spot on earth.

These dreams of empire were not only selfish but impractical. The U.S. Department of Agriculture had already tested the possibilities of cattle raising on Kodiak. Grain had failed to mature and it was necessary to have winter feed shipped up from Seattle. Haymaking was nearly impossible. The expense of maintaining an experimental herd was extreme and the cattle were taken back to the mainland. The vision of Admiralty as lumbering country was equally ridiculous. One quick destructive cutting would have been all that steep-sloped northern island could offer. Erosion would have prevented the trees from seeding back.

The livestock men laid siege to the land of the brownie first. Ever since the Game Laws had blocked their plans, they had been carrying on an unending campaign to stir up public fear and hatred of the brownies. When Thayer was killed by a bear and the story of his death was given space in all newspapers, the livestock men decided public opinion was in as favorable a climate for their own special interests as it would ever be and made their attack.

For reasons known only to its members the Game Commission buckled quickly under pressure. The Game Laws were revised. After July 1, 1930, it was announced, any brownie or silvertip found within one mile of a human habitation anywhere throughout Alaska could be killed at any time of year. On Kodiak Island a resident could kill a bear any time he considered it a menace.

Within a year the lumbering industry made its bid. A sizable fifty-year contract for timber cutting on Admiralty Island and nearby areas was awarded. Here too all protective laws were canceled.

At that moment the brownie was being protected only against nonresidents. With civilization storming his last two strongholds, his chances looked very slim.

The fact that the biggest bear on earth still exists today is due strictly to the efforts of conservation groups here in the States and the handful of men who led them. Writers like Stuart Edward White and statesmen like Senator Arthur Capper took up the cause of the brownie and threw themselves into a bitter fight to save him. Organizations like the American Society of Mammalogists, the Boone and Crockett Club and the New York Zoological Society angrily protested the revision of the Game Laws and demanded that Kodiak and Admiralty be set aside as sanctuaries. When the news came down from the Territory that hired brigades of riflemen were being organized to exterminate the bears on these islands, the battle became frantic and desperate.

The first major victory came in 1933, when President Roosevelt repudiated the timber-cutting contract for Admiralty Island and ordered the Department of the Interior to study the region's possibilities as a national park. Others followed, most of them compromises. The interior of Kodiak Island was set aside as a federal game-management area with controlled hunting. A mile-wide strip of the coastline was reserved for the salmon industry. A few sections of Admiralty, totaling little more than 80 square miles out of the island's 2000, were made into a sanctuary. In 1941, when Secretary of the Interior Harold Ickes turned in a report strongly urging that Admiralty be made a national monument, the future of the great brown bear seemed permanently secure.

Now, a very few years later, the brownie is more urgently in need of help from conservationists than he was back in 1931, and closer to extinction than he has ever been throughout the ten thousand or more centuries of his existence.

176

On Kodiak Island the situation is bad but not yet critical. Cattlemen have moved onto the land that was reserved for the salmon industry and are whittling away at the interior by a variety of devious means. Sheepmen are on their way in right now. It is no exaggeration to say that most livestock owners illegally kill bears whenever the opportunity presents itself. Kodiak is public land, but the political power of the men who wish to convert it into free private pasture is formidable. As recently as 1951, the Alaska Legislature passed a resolution demanding that all protection be removed from the bears on Kodiak.

The salmon fishermen have been suffering from their own greed and finding their waters depleted. Salmon traps, which are illegal in Canada, are most likely responsible for this. But the fishermen believe the brownies are eating too many salmon. The practice of sniping at them from the safety of fishing boats has become widespread.

The brownies might conceivably hold out against sniping fishermen and poaching stockmen on Kodiak for a few years to come. But across the Gulf, on Admiralty Island, the end is very near.

President Roosevelt's plans to make this scenic wilderness paradise a national park were laid aside during the war and ignored completely by his successors after his death. Now, once again, Admiralty's value is being reckoned solely in terms of pulpwood prices. In 1956 two contracts were granted, each of them remarkably similar to the lumbering concession that was repudiated back in 1933. The Georgia Pacific Corporation of Portland, Oregon, and the Alaska Lumber and Pulp Company of Tokyo, Japan, were given permission to cut a total of 14 billion board feet of timber on Admiralty and the surrounding area, nearly one-fifth of all the timber in the Tongass National Forest, our largest remaining stretch of wilderness.

Very recently the National Association of Wild Life Conservationists raised two very interesting questions concerning these contracts, questions that should not remain unanswered.

177

Why were such large and long-term concessions granted without sealed competitive bids being made?

Why is the U.S. government selling, for approximately twenty-five million dollars, a quantity and quality of timber for which the Canadian government would ask at least seventy-five million in adjacent British Columbia?

The basic question, however, is whether or not the American people are willing to give up their biggest stretch of true wild land and one of their greatest game animals to provide a source of raw material for Japan's textile industry. Legislation is now being introduced to block the schemes of the pulpwood barons by having Admiralty Island made a national park, sponsored by Senators Aiken of Vermont and Anderson of New Mexico. The fate of such legislation will depend entirely on public support and interest . . . or the lack of it.

There can be absolutely no doubt that allowing the contracted amount of timber to be cut will permanently destroy the steep-sloped island, since erosion and flooding will be direct and immediate results. Even if the brown bears could survive the large-scale invasion of the lumbermen, which is unlikely, they could never survive the flooding of the salmon's spawning beds. When the silvery horde no longer swarms in from the sea, the brownie's means of life will be gone.

Alaska needs new fields of employment now that the salmon boats have fished out their waters. Pulp mills and lumbering camps seem to provide a ready answer. But sacrificing the Territory's hunting as a result is most certainly no solution. A well-managed big-game population is the most vital segment of Alaska's future economy. The sportsman-tourist industry is big business, outranked only by mining now that commercial fishing has dwindled. Thirty thousand hunters, fishermen and tourists visit southeastern Alaska each year. They'll hardly be coming north to see scalped mountainsides and smell the fumes of pulp mills. There are fifteen to twenty million potential big-game hunters in this country, men who are contenting themselves with close-to-home white-tail deer and dreaming of Alaska. A steadily

178

increasing standard of living and longer vacations are going to send more and more of them up each year, if the Territory's game animals are still there to attract them.

Successful handling of wildlife resources is very much like the handling of any sort of investment. You have to learn to live off the interest and let the capital remain. I can foresee a time when the great trophy animals like the brownie, the silvertip and the polar bear are going to have to be rationed out one per hunter per lifetime. And I can see no reason why any man should kill more than one. I can also see no reason why the bear population need ever be reduced to a level where any future hunter is denied his chance.

But the history of this country has been a chronicle of senseless waste of all game animals. It has been said that the only way of predicting the future is by examining the past. If this is true, the brown bear is doomed.

Somewhere in the high country of Admiralty Island a brownie is preparing for the long winter sleep. Far beneath his mountain heights the spruce forests and rye meadows are flowing together in shadow, for autumn nights come early in the North. When this shaggy giant finally picks his den and beds down, his respiration will gradually dwindle to a rate of no more than one faint breath each 12 or 15 seconds and his heartbeat will slow correspondingly. His stomach will shrink to a mere fraction of its normal size and his awareness of the outside world will vary between deep sleep and semiconsciousness. If he is a very large bear he may have done this thirty or forty times in his life, trusting each time that the world in which he has a place and a purpose will not change.

When he emerges from hibernation next April or May, as groggy and grouchy as a human being before his morning coffee, will the wilderness still be there? Or will the spruces be ravaged, with melting snow already beginning to erode the slopes, and the meadows dotted with the shacks of lumbering camps? Will springtime in the northern wilds be the same season of renewal and rebirth it has always been? Or will he find brigades of hired riflemen seeking him out above the timberline while his senses are still dulled, and pass through scatterings of poison baits on his way down to the coast to wait for salmon runs that will never come again?

It is impossible to watch without regret as he goes the way of the bison and the sea-otter—one more vanishing American that coming generations will find only in textbooks and museums. Here is the largest carnivore on earth, one of the mightiest that has ever lived, an actual relic of the Ice Age—hovering on the verge of extinction because a few little men have respect for neither the future nor the past.

If he passes he will go proudly. No one has ever yet seen a brownie die a cringing and cowardly death.

BOOK THREE　The Big Cats

XIII

THE BIG SPOTTED CAT

In a dense section of a great southern jungle-forest, a band of white-lipped peccaries were feeding. The sun had just gone down. The sounds of stirring wildlife were beginning to fill the hushed cover, recently steamed by burning light. The wild pigs moved noisily through the thickness, eating everything, grubbing out roots and insects, robbing birds' nests, stripping berry bushes. There is no lack of food in the tropics. The hot wet earth spawns growth, accelerates it, animal and vegetable alike. The plant life crowds together, battles for space and sunlight. Trees a hundred yards tall form the pillars of the rain forest, their trunks and branches covered with parasite vines. Smaller trees grow beneath these branches, seeking the filtered sun. And on the forest floor, grasses and mosses and small ferns compete for the minute amounts of light that trickles down.

Among the animals, this battle for existence is every bit as intense. Fifty yards ahead of the leaders of the peccary band, a great yellow-and-black cat rose suddenly from his hiding place. He was a thing of beauty as he gathered his hind legs beneath him. A stocky cat with a large head and mighty jaws, his fine hide was covered with black-spotted rosettes, distinct on the yellow. But like many of Nature's most ornamental creatures, he was a thing of deadliness. He made one quick short jump to get clear of the thicket, then streaked through the cover.

The little pig he'd selected had no chance to run. It whirled about to face the attack, but one lightning-fast smash of the big cat's claws snapped its neck and left it shuddering and jerking

on the ground. The cat pinned it down and snarled at the others. The grunting sounds they had made while feeding gave way to deep sharp notes of alarm. The hair rose on their backs and they scooted off rapidly through the brush. The odor they left behind, when fear opened their scent glands, was distinct and very strong in the still wet air.

When the sounds of their escape dwindled in the distance, the big cat lowered his head and picked up his kill. Just as a housecat carries off a mouse, he trotted away with the dead pig. He entered the thicket where he'd lain in wait. And there, secure in silence, he began to feed.

In a little less than an hour, he'd had his fill. He moved away from the carcass, sat back on his haunches and began washing himself. Slowly and carefully he cleaned the blood from every bit of the fur that his tongue could reach. Then, wetting his paw, he went to work on the rest of his hide. When he was finished, he arched his back and stretched himself. The pleasure, the contentment that came with a good meal, was obvious in all his movements.

Suddenly he froze very still. His ears flicked slightly, as if straining to hear. Something strange and unknown, something out of place in the jungle, had made a sound in the distance. The cat waited a long time. Noises of movement came again.

He turned and ghosted rapidly away through the fading light. He was not really afraid, as yet, but his composure had been shattered. He wanted to put a wide stretch of thick jungle cover between himself and whatever it was he had heard.

In the last few minutes before the gloom gave way to pitch blackness, five men entered the thicket where the peccary band had been feeding. Four of them were jungle Indians and their clothes were scanty arrangements of rags and ornaments. Between them, they held on leash a pack of a dozen mongrel dogs. Most of these were extremely small and thin-boned animals that seemed to be constantly shivering in spite of the heat. These dogs had been trailing, in silence and apparently without enthusiasm, the twelve-hour-old line the cat had left when it had come to this thicket to sleep.

The fifth man was darker than the Indians but his features were those of a half-breed. He wore khakis and hunting boots but he was bare-headed. He was an extremely powerful man, with a great chest and shockingly wide shoulders. He looked for all the world like a wealthy hunter with a small safari. But he carried no rifle, only a ten-foot hardwood spear that tapered smoothly to a perfect point.

The dogs coursed their way over and discovered the remains of the peccary. They began making low, whining sounds. One of the Indians pushed the brush aside and stared for a long time through the near-darkness.

"*Jaguara!*" he called over, his voice low and fearful.

The fully-clothed man lay down his spear and worked his way through the thicket. He looked at the freshly-killed pig while he lit a long, thin cigar. Then he smiled broadly.

"*El tigre!*" he exclaimed softly.

He was one of a strange race of men called *tigreros*, men whose feeling and instincts have become more in tune with the sensitivities of the big predators than with the standards of civilization. He was an educated man, a man with a certain amount of wealth and position in his country. Hunting had merely been a hobby with him through the many years he'd carried a rifle. But now, ever since he'd discovered for himself the strange and highly-skilled sport of killing the giant jungle jaguars with a spear, hunting had become an obsession.

He had speared his first jaguar in comparative safety. Two companions had been stationed at either side with high-powered rifles aimed and ready. But he had felt very much alone as he'd matched his strength against the death-thrashing of the big cat impaled on his spear. And when that first hunt had been successful, when he'd stood above that trophy carcass, a strange new feeling had swept over him and he'd heard nothing his companions had said to him. The feeling was a sort of catharsis, a cleansing emotion that swept through him and tingled along

186

every nerve in his body, a rich new kind of exultation with overtones of sadness. In all his years of rifle hunting he had never known such a feeling.

So now the man was a *tigrero*, dedicated to the one sport beside which all others seemed tame. And now, when he hunted, he hunted with his feelings and not his thoughts. An emotion that was deeper, older, more basic than excitement sent him along the trails of the great spotted cats.

He sat back against a tree while his men made camp for the night. He looked calm, enjoying a cigar and seemingly relaxing. But there was a place beside his temples where the blood raced in and out.

The jaguar kept on the move throughout most of the night. He was not hunting now and after a few miles of jungle were behind him he forgot about being disturbed and his wanderings became aimless and desultory. Several times through the dark hours he stalked different jungle creatures and pounced, merely to frighten them.

This was a game with the big cat, but it was also more than that. He was enjoying himself, thrilling in his skill and ability, just as he trotted great distances without reason to enjoy his own strength, the ripple and play of mighty muscles under the bright fur.

He'd been born to rule this jungle, born to a heritage of mastery. He was one of a giant race of jaguars and he weighed almost three hundred pounds. His species has a characteristic that is extremely rare among mammals. The size of jaguars is not determined by the location of their range. A race of gigantic jaguars may live next to a race of small jaguars. In the jungles beyond the nearby mountains the spotted cats were constantly harassed by pumas. But here in this cover the jaguar's rule was undisputed.

This jaguar had been born with one litter mate in a thicket of this same jungle. At the northern and southern ends of jaguar country, the females den up like pumas and the kittens are born in the springtime, but in the unchanging jungle a litter may come at any time of year. This jaguar had never seen his father. Actually, the big male was one of the dangers his mother had guarded against. Father jaguars invariably kill the young if they are unprotected.

His childhood had been long. The spots with which he'd been born had changed slowly to rosettes, his brown hide had ripened to gold. His mother had taught him how to hunt, how to care for himself for nearly two years. Then she'd suddenly turned on her kittens and driven them off. She'd been ready to mate again.

The jaguar had remained with his brother for only a very short time. A dispute over a freshly-killed monkey had become a vicious, deadly battle and he'd driven his brother off with slashes in the yellow and black satin skin that would remain scars for life. That had been five years ago. Since then, this cat had lived the lonely life he preferred. Except for brief matings with no regularity to them, he did not seek the company of others of his kind. If he mated twice with the same female, this was accidental.

When early morning sunlight began filtering through the massive trees, his wanderings ceased. He drank deeply at a slow-moving, near-stagnant jungle stream, then moved into a thicket on its banks. He lay on his side to sleep, twitching only slightly when the flies found him.

He woke up all at once. Something was moving on the mudflats beneath him.

Soundlessly, he rolled up and lay still with his chest against the ground. The wet slithering sound came again. He began creeping out of the growth, inching his way along, gliding through the thickness and blending in with the scattered splotches of liquid noon sunlight and the spangled leaf shadows. As slowly as a shadow moves, his head came through the bushes that edged the mudflats.

188

Not ten yards away, a ten-foot-long reptile was crawling over the hard sunbaked mud— *jacaré*, the jungle crocodile, an ancient enemy of the jaguar race. The big cat waited at the end of the cover. Only his eyes moved.

The crocodile waddled about until it faced the river. It slid forward a little to ease its weight into a comfortable depression in the baked mud-crust. Then it lay still, enjoying the sun that now burned from directly above.

The jaguar waited in his hiding place for nearly an hour. The flies found him once more but he endured them and made no move that would betray his presence. He gave the big reptile enough time in the sun to sink into a near-stupor of contentment.

Then he bounded over the hard crust and pounced. Both of his great front paws smashed down on the heavy-scaled neck with bone-crushing force and the full length of his claws dug in. His hind legs raked down along the crocodile's sides until they found a spot that gave way. Then they tore into the hide furiously. His big white fangs clamped down on the armored neck, bit hard and sheared their way through.

The crocodile exploded back to life. Its jaws flew open and it tried to turn its head, but the clamping of the jaguar's teeth and the vise-grip of his paws was too strong. It swung its heavy, sharp-edged tail around in a blow that would have felled a small tree, but the big cat crouched low and held fast. The crocodile thrashed and twisted again and again. Finally its frantic efforts turned it over sideways.

This was what the jaguar was waiting for. He broke suddenly free, pounced again and the big reptile lay helpless on its back while he ripped it open.

He stepped back and waited while the jerking, shuddering movements of death slowed. Motion finally ceased in the crocodile's body. Even then, he stood still a few minutes longer and regarded the thing he had killed with expressionless eyes. He stepped up and sniffed it once, then turned back toward his thicket.

Jaguars are fond of alligator and crocodile meat, but this cat was not yet hungry again. His kill would be here when he wanted it. He would be near enough to discourage any scavengers.

Back at his sleeping spot once more, he went through the entire painstaking ritual of washing himself again. Then he settled back on his side in the growth.

The second time he woke the late afternoon sunlight was streaming across through the trees on the far side of the river. He rolled up and then lay very still and searched the thicket with his eyes. A feeling that something was wrong hung in the air.

Nothing moved through the shadowy patterns of intertangled growth. But from the mudflats there came a hushed murmur of voices of men, a subdued whine of impatience made by a hunting dog. The jaguar had never heard any of these sounds before. He was still not afraid but he was wary of the unknown.

He started back toward the thicket, back toward the jungle. But suddenly shrill voices exploded behind him. The dogs had found the dead crocodile and were running the line back to his sleeping place. Their size let them dash through the thicket as though it were a clearing.

The big cat turned to fight. But these unknown creatures made no move to attack him. They merely swarmed about him and screamed as though they were in pain. He turned and tried to pounce on one, but in the dense cover it escaped him easily. He leaped at another with no better success.

He was still not afraid. These creatures were merely an annoyance, like the jungle's many pestering and biting insects. He turned and hurried back toward the mudflats. In the open, he knew, he could catch these things, catch them and rip them to lifeless shreds.

At the edge of the cover he stopped. The men were waiting by the dead crocodile. For a few seconds a terrible fear, the wild things' fear of the trap, shuddered over him. But it gave way to anger. He had been lord of this jungle throughout his lifetime. The dogs were still shrieking behind him.

He stepped into the open and started toward the men.

The *tigrero* waved the Indians back, but they were already moving away, moving slowly so as not to invite a charge. He shook his spear a little, making sure he alone kept the giant cat's attention. The jaguar's trot gave way to a bounding, charging run.

The *tigrero* waited for the right moment to plant his spear, watching the big cat's feet. Time stood still for him now and he was alone in this contest. Nothing in the world mattered, existed or had meaning but himself and the giant jaguar. He felt all-powerful now and certain of the outcome.

He waited until the great spotted cat was perhaps ten yards away. Then he shoved the base of the spear into the ground and aimed the point.

The jaguar made one last bound and then sprang. This creature that dare face him was new and unknown, but his anger destroyed all fear. He meant to crash down with his paws on the man's shoulders, grip with claw and fang and then rake hard with his hind legs.

But all at once, in mid-air, there was a terrible shock. A burning pain drove through him just inside his left fore-leg. Six feet short of the man he came abruptly to the ground again. He clawed and bit at the hardwood shaft on which he was impaled, but he could not break it. The man was lifting it, twisting it, trying to flip him on his back.

Suddenly the jaguar realized that this was his enemy, not the spear or the dogs. This was his tormentor, the cause of the terrible pain that numbed his side. He stopped fighting the pole and started fighting to get at the man. His feet churned at the hardened mud, his body slid forward inch by inch. The spear was tapered and, as he slid farther and farther along it, the pain in his side magnified itself. But every remaining bit of his strength was concentrated on getting closer, getting at the thing that was destroying him.

The *tigrero* tried in vain to get the cat's feet away from the ground. The weight of the jaguar was too great. The man could not turn and run. His only chance of life lay in keeping his grip on the spear.

With an effort that very nearly killed him, the jaguar lunged and closed the remaining distance. His side was torn wide open, but the claws of one forepaw reached his tormentor and pulled him into reach of his fangs. His weight bore the man to the ground, his teeth ripped and crushed through bone.

The big cat rose to face new enemies but none were there. The Indians were backing off through the brush, calling to the dogs, who were hesitating, but still keeping well away from him.

His leg went out from under him and he dragged himself through the jungle, a great yellow and black cat with a ten-foot spear through him. His life was pouring from him fast. The first tree caught the spear and stopped him. He fell, but his jaws were still parted, a low snarl still warning the world he could be dangerous.

Shadows were lengthening on the river. In the dim shallows, just beyond the edge of the last mudbanks, his old enemies the crocodiles watched him and waited.

XIV

THE TURNING POINT

THE puma came down through the timbered ridges at a
frantic run, bounding like a creature of madness. Fear surged
and bubbled through his insides. Fear burned at his mind like
fever. He hit the canyon floor, bounding lightly on great furred-
muscle legs, then shot across the flat stretches of sparse cover
directly toward the forbidding wall of the sierra.

A hound's voice rang faintly, one voice far back in the distance
of the lonely ridge country. The voice came again, closer and
nearer, and another voice answered. Between the steadily-ringing
notes of their baying, other hound cries were appearing in
faintness. The pack was still with him. None of the tricks he'd
used in the timber had shaken them.

The big, long-tailed, dun-colored cat hit the sheer wall of
rock and sprang straight up. He huddled on a narrow, rounded
ledge for the split-second needed to regain his balance, then
ran a few steps and leaped again. He went on up the face of the
sierra in a series of impossible leaps from one dizzying, precarious clawhold to another. And yet he looked effortless in his
speedy climb straight into the sky. Beneath him the canyon
floor dropped farther and farther away.

The blood-singing of the dogs below steadied itself and grew,
nearer, louder, more savage, clashing and earth-shaking. Triumph was in the baying, the arrogance of certainty. They
thought he was trapped in the canyon. They thought they had
him, that he'd turn at bay before the sierra.

A solid stream of dogs splashed out of the timber and poured across the ground in full cry. Blueticks and black and tans, they were, hounds of many breeds and many colors. And yet the pack seemed a single living thing as it drove toward the canyon wall, much like a human mob.

But abruptly, the hound voices cut out in the still air. The dogs smiled about uncertainly at the bottom of the sierra wall, whining softly in frustration. The pack was gone. Only individual hounds, baffled and suddenly tired, were left.

High and safe in the rocks, the puma watched them. His sides were still once more. His heavy breathing had stopped. And yet the fear stayed with him, an intense and biting fear. He glared at the dogs far below and spat with hatred. He could leap out from the ledge, he knew, bound down to drop suddenly in their midst and scatter them like deer. They themselves were nothing to fear.

A horse dodged out of the trees and galloped toward them, its rider urging it into a run. The big cat flattened himself even more, tried to become a part of the ledge. This was the thing he feared, the creature that could kill at a distance. This was Death that came with nothing near, no animal to battle, no chance to fight for life. Fear became a maddening, tightening pain within him.

Three feelings had governed this creature, who is also called cougar or panther or lion, throughout thirteen years of staying alive. There was the mating urge that sent him searching when spring warmed the rocks and scented the earth. There was hunger, the hunger that made him the hunter he was. But his strongest feeling was fear, fear of man. This was his lifetime burden and it determined his every movement. It made him feel naked in bright daylight or open country. It ruled each step he took.

The man on the canyon floor dismounted and walked over to stand among the defeated hounds, looking over every foot of the sierra face. But the puma's steel muscles held back the terror within him. Finally the man shook his head and turned back to his horse. A tired procession began the slow backtracking of what had been a fast and furious chase.

Night was coming. Sunlight streamed up toward the bare-rock Arizona peaks like a battery of giant searchlights.

Two hours later, in full darkness, the big cat moved.

He rose to a sitting position and, stirring cautiously, looked down through the night. Then he arched and stretched himself and began the long trip to the canyon floor. He reached cover, stopped to look and listen, then hurried on west in the pitch-black moon-shadow of the cliff. The spot had been disturbed. He had to leave it far behind.

Well before midnight, he made his kill.

He snaked his way into the rocks and lay still when he heard movement in the brush on the other side of the canyon. There were three deer, a doe with a fawn and a young spikehorn. The doe moved carefully and fearfully, in quick decisive spurts. The fawn stayed close. But the young buck wandered about, impatient to reach the creek. The deer passed fifty yards from the puma's hiding place. The spikehorn drifted aimlessly to the right and closer.

The big cat took two short, tight bounds to get speed, then shot across the open like a rifle bullet. The young buck didn't quite have time to turn his head and see the thing that killed him.

With the contentment of weight in his stomach, the puma trotted to the creek to drink and then began the slow and careful task of washing himself. He cleaned his forepaws and then wiped away at the dried blood on his neck and ears, exactly like a housecat does. Then he started following the canyon west once more. He was going nowhere in particular. He was wandering now, a slight bounce in his step, his head swinging from side to side, his long tail waving up and down.

By early morning, just before the moon disappeared, he was crossing a high plateau that nestled among the peaks. It was here that he discovered the strange tracks.

He scented them once, then lifted his head and surveyed the horizon. Nothing moved through lonely distances. He lowered his muzzle again to the track but he couldn't identify it. It was the trail of a creature he had never before encountered in these mountains. The scent told him two things. This was the track of a cat, a large cat. But the creature was not of his own species.

If it had been daylight he could have seen the flatlands that reached toward the Mexican border. Had he known anything of boundaries, he might have reasoned that the stranger was a visitor from another country. But he knew only his own world. And among wild things he held himself supreme, he feared nothing but man.

He let out a tight whining growl and began tracking the line of the invader.

The trail wandered aimlessly, north to the brink of the sierra, west into the canyons, then suddenly back toward the timbered low country. Nowhere did the stranger stop to feed or lie up. The scent did not strengthen. The line was still twelve hours old when the puma left it. The false dawn had come to the sky above the peaks and caught him unaware. The feeling of nakedness crept along his hide like vermin as the light grew in the air. This was country where men hunted. The puma forgot the trail of the strange invading cat entirely, remembered only the fear that ruled his life. He stopped suddenly and slunk away to seek a hiding place in the rocks.

The puma woke only when the late afternoon sunlight trickled in to reach him. He climbed out to sun himself a few minutes, then washed himself completely once more. He stood up and stretched, slowly and with pleasure. Then he began working his way down to drink at the creek. He had forgotten entirely the invader he had hunted so earnestly the night before.

Not for long. He was returning to his kill when a wind-scent snapped back his memory. Dodging immediately into the creek-growth he snaked a silent way along, each sense keyed up in readiness.

The stranger was feeding on the spikehorn—a great yellow and black spotted cat, much larger than the puma. This lion had no way of knowing a jaguar, for never before in his lifetime had one migrated as far north as these mountains. But he did know he feared nothing except man, that no wild creature was allowed to rob him of a kill.

The puma edged steadily closer and waited for a moment when the jaguar's head was buried in the deer's lungs cavity. Then, in an abrupt, unbelievably fast rush, he attacked.

The fight exploded again as the jaguar lunged, its fangs snapping. The spotted cat, slashing him now, was bleeding.

He smashed down on the spotted back, dug in and held with ripping fang and claw as they rolled over and over across the canyon floor. The jaguar finally broke free, dodged back and faced him, its surprise changing to anger. It began moving in, slowly and steadily, stalking him. He circled wide to await another chance.

The fight exploded again as the jaguar lunged, its fangs

snapping and the puma dodged and slapped with both paws, then leaped away, circling once more. First blood was the puma's. The great spotted cat, slashing him now, was bleeding from a slashed shoulder.

The puma snarled and spat steadily as he moved, twisting and feinting to avoid being cornered against the rocks. The jaguar stalked in silence, its shoulders and jaws as tense as a diamondback's striking-coil. It lunged again and the snarl of the lion reached a new pitch as he met this charge, rising on his hind legs, striking and slashing. He leaped clear and circled again, still unhurt. The jaguar moved toward him, new cuts on its head and neck.

Again the jaguar lunged and this time the puma met him squarely, shoulder against shoulder, fang against fang. Then, kicking and screaming, the lion went down. One side of the jaguar's head was solid blood, the eye gone and the ear a stump. But he had a neck hold and he kept it. The puma slashed and clawed, but the jaguar held on.

Twisting and rolling, the lion fought like a hooked trout, trying to break the terrible vise-grip on its neck. The jaguar was massive and powerful, but the frantic fight of the lighter cat kept him off balance. They crashed into the rocks, a swirling mass of tan and gold, a flurry of fang and striking claw. And the puma leaped free.

He circled wide now, his snarl almost a whine. A great tear in his tawny hide hung loose and bared the bone of his shoulder. The blood fell in large drops—dark, almost black, on the bare rock.

The jaguar crashed in again. The lion reared and struck with his forepaws, then met the charge and went down under the weight of the spotted cat's shoulders. There was another tangle and then the grinding crunch of bone as they rolled over. But the puma was suddenly up and clear.

The jaguar faced him on three legs.

The lion began wheeling in and slashing, trying to send the jaguar down. Each time he ripped by, the fangs of the stranger

198

snapped on empty air like a pistol shot. But the end had begun for the jaguar. Finally, it turned too quickly, stumbled and went down. Immediately the puma pounced, attacking with no more caution than he'd use in butchering a deer. When he stepped back the jaguar lay still.

The lion stared at his dead enemy. He was breathing hard and bleeding fast, but the pleasure of victory, the realization of his own strength and fighting ability, was stronger than pain or exhaustion. He was king of these mountains. He had proven it again.

Suddenly and unexpectedly, less than two hundred yards away, the baying of an entire hound pack exploded in the twilight stillness. The puma froze a second, held by a blood-chilling wave of fear. Then he bolted up into the rocks. On a ledge thirty feet above the canyon floor he lay still. He dared show movement no longer.

Anger was mixed with his fear now, and something akin to a human sense of unfairness. Bloody and exhausted, this was no time for being hunted, no time for the horror of the chase. This feeling grew inside him as the hound pack came on in full cry, running the trail he'd left when he'd stalked the jaguar.

The dogs were directly below him now, sending their challenge echoing up through the rocks. A horse galloped up and a man leaped from the saddle, facing the cliff wall with his rifle held ready at his shoulder.

The old fear, the fear that had shaped his life, was pulsing through the puma's veins. But the new feeling stayed and grew stronger. And something was changing within him as he lay still and watched the man.

He was thirteen years old. Thirteen times the seasons had circled while he had matched the skill of the hunter against the wild world and won. He'd killed the biggest bulls of the elk herds. The giant mountain coyotes had run before him. He had driven black bear from his canyons. He'd taken on a strange spotted cat nearly twice his size in a battle to the death and won. He'd been born to hunt, not to be hunted.

But for thirteen years he'd lived on a tightrope. He'd run from hounds when he'd known full well a few swipes of his claws would leave them broken and yelping. He'd moved about only in darkness, although he loved the warmth of the sun on his hide. He'd kept to the thickest cover and the highest mountain reaches. He'd been created a hunter and yet he'd lived the life of a skulking hunted outlaw. And all because of the fear, the fear he'd drunk in his mother's milk, the fear of the creature beneath him now—the strange and puzzling thing that could kill at a distance.

The distance was short this time—very short.

Something snapped inside him. Something broke loose. One hundred and thirty pounds of solid muscle revolted. He sprang from the ledge and streaked through the rocks.

At the sound of the first rifle shot his lungs exploded in scalding wetness and he somersaulted down to crash on the canyon floor, but he got his feet beneath him and kept on going. All of him—pain, sickness, hatred and every ounce of his strength had tightened into absolute concentration on charging, on getting the thing that hunted him. The second shot smashed him in the mouth in mid-air, a ripping crash that dimmed his consciousness like a candle in wind, but he reached the man in that final spring and he could still see his forepaws. One savage flurry and this creature that he had feared all his life lay limp on the ground.

Vaguely, the puma felt surprised. The thing had died so easily! But then the hounds were upon him, tearing at his flanks. He started to fight back but strength was draining away with his blood. Forcing movement over the terrible sick-wet pain inside him, he turned and bounded back for the safety of the rocks.

He lay still on the ledge. There was no exultation now, no sense of victory. He was drowning in his own blood and he could no longer rise to his feet. The world darkened in his eyes, the clamor of hounds dimmed in his ears. He snarled once, defying Death as another invader, another enemy.

Jerking and twitching spasmodically, his great muscles lived on for several minutes after his mind was gone.

XV

TO THE DEATH

In the spring of 1914, two prospectors were working out a placer claim, not far from Murray, Idaho. The stream in which they hoped to find gold ran down the floor of a canyon sided by near-perpendicular walls.

A female puma had her kittens denned in the rocks a little more than halfway up one of these walls. The two miners had known she was there for several days now. They'd seen the mother cat several times, heard the cries of her whelps.

It had become quite obvious to the prospectors that they were never going to get rich from this particular mountain stream. They knew there was a ready market for baby lions, that zoological parks and animal dealers were paying good prices. For some time they'd been thinking of shooting the big female cat and robbing her den.

They were discussing this one afternoon when one of them grabbed the other's arm and pointed up at the outline of the cliff against the sky. Something had moved up there.

It wasn't the puma. They were certain of that. They'd seen her already that day, slinking back to her den. She wouldn't be leaving the kittens in bright daylight, not with them working just below.

They kept on watching the top of the canyon wall. There was just the suggestion of movement among the big rocks that were like tombstones in a graveyard of giants. Then the creature came into full view, silhouetted against the skyline, caught in the full blaze of bright sunlight.

It was a grizzly.

The bear moved on along the rim. He could have been dark gray or black. What looked like a tinge of light hair on his back might merely have been sunlight. But there were other things that made the miners certain he wasn't a black bear. His shoulders were high. The hump there was unmistakable. His head was much larger than that of a black bear. No, he was a grizzly all right.

He was almost directly above them now and no bear had ever looked bigger. His head was carried high and he walked steadily on with a gait that revealed his great weight and yet seemed poised and delicate. He was going somewhere, perhaps returning to a kill.

Suddenly, he stopped. The prospectors stood rock-still beside the water and held their breath. But the bear was past them now and he didn't look back. He waited there for about thirty seconds, testing the air and searching the canyon ahead of him.

Then, as suddenly as he'd stopped, he started again, moving over the rim and down along the first of the series of ridges that jutted like a staircase from the sheer face of the cliff.

They watched his progress for a few more seconds. Then, abruptly, they realized what was happening.

He was going to pass directly in front of the mouth of the cat's den!

The mother lion had seen the grizzly, too. She'd gone to the entrance of her cave to check once more on the security of her home, to make sure the men she'd seen on the stream were coming no nearer. Satisfied, she'd been about to start back to her kittens when her eyes caught movement far above. Not two hundred yards away, the giant bear was coming down the slope toward her, his weight speeding up his progress on the grade.

The puma backed away, crouched low, turned and glanced once at her kittens. There were three of the baby lions. They were about ten days old, their eyes just beginning to open. They looked nothing like their mother. Their tails were short and ringed, their hides spotted. Playing together, shrieking as they wrestled and scratched and bit at each other, they had no thought of danger. As yet, they had no knowledge of fear.

Their world was completely secure. The big mother lion was with them always in the daylight hours. Her hunting trips were short at whelping time. Only in the safety of complete darkness did she leave them, slipping up over the rim on silent pads, using all of her skill as a hunter to make a quick kill, feed rapidly and hurry back.

No, fear had not yet come into the lives of the kittens. Fear was for their mother to know. She looked at them a moment longer, then slipped back to crouch beside a rock and watch the ledge. The grizzly was little more than a hundred yards off, coming on steadily.

The puma dodged back. Hidden by the rocks, she sprang straight up, catching herself and huddling for a second on an outcropping to regain her balance, then leaping again. On the ledge above her den, she flattened herself and then snaked forward. She seemed a part of the rock now. Nothing moved but her eyes.

The great bear came on, never slowing. He was close enough so she could see the little eyes in the long tapered face.

The lion backed up to a sitting position, then took a short tight bound to gather speed and shot into the air. She smashed down on the great shaggy neck, dug in and held with fang and ripping claw as the grizzly stumbled and almost went down. Her powerful hind legs dug furrows in his flanks as he reared up with a righteous bawling roar and tried to shake her free. She hooked her front paws even more deeply as he sat down and tried to reach her with his massive arms.

But when he rolled on over, trying to smash her against the rock with his full weight, she let go and leaped lightly away. Then she turned and faced him, ahead of him on the ledge, her body close to the cliff wall.

She snarled and spat constantly, her face twisting and threatening. Actually, though, she did not want to fight. She merely

203

wanted him to turn and go back. All she knew was that she could not allow him to pass that close to her kittens.

But the big silvertip had never turned aside for any other creature of the wild. He stood still and watched the puma for a few seconds, while the frozen surprise and bewilderment inside him melted to anger. Then, with a great roar, he charged.

A bear charges on all fours and fights an offensive battle with his jaws. Only when cornered or at bay does he go back on his hind legs and strike with his paws. Bear hugs were invented by men. The grizzly drove the puma back along the ledge with a series of short rushes, biting and snapping. The lion defended herself by flailing away with her claws as she retreated. The battle looked very much like a dog pestering a house-cat, magnified many times in size and deadliness.

Inch by inch, the lion gave ground. The big bear kept up his attack, certain of the outcome. Even in the heat of battle he caught the scent of the den and realized why the lion had attacked. Had he scented the den sooner, he would have made a wide detour and the fight would never have occurred. But it was too late now for him to do anything but keep on, carry the battle to the puma until she either fled or he killed her.

He charged again, but the cat would not retreat past the den. She crouched against the cliff wall, looking small and huddled, then came alive and shot directly for his throat.

The grizzly took a step backward and reared up, wavering for a second on the brink of that ledge. Then he swung back and smashed down, trying to trap the lion within the deadly circle of his teeth and claws. But she was suddenly free, waiting for him on the ledge once more.

He moved forward more slowly. So far he'd been fighting in blind anger, but he could fight with caution and cunning as well. There was no more lunging as he closed the distance between them. He kept all four feet solidly planted, advancing with quick short steps. The puma was staying between him and the cliff wall, gliding back and forth, feinting occasionally by striking at the air.

Suddenly, he wheeled past her and turned. Now he was standing firm between her and her den. He'd force her to charge. And she'd be charging certain death.

She hesitated but a second. Then, with a loud cry, she sprang. The grizzly went back on his hind legs with his heavy paws flailing, but the cat's speed carried her through the swinging claws. She sank her long fangs into his face and held on, clawing his neck while her hind feet raked his stomach.

The great bear smashed at her, tore at her, and felt her bones break beneath his paws. But he was blinded with blood and pain. His balance was gone. Abruptly, the firm rock went out from beneath his feet. He felt the sickening sensation of falling even above the pain.

The prospectors stood still, speechless, as the battling bear and cat hit the last tier of ledges, thrashing wildly but locked tightly together, then slid off to fall a hundred feet through the air and crash into the branches of the jackpines far down the canyon.

There was no further sound, no sign of movement. The men stared at the spot where the two fighters had disappeared for a long time.

They knew they'd seen something very, very rare. And they wondered what freak of chance, what defiance of the laws of probability had caused the big bear to move directly past the big cat's den at whelping time, the only time she would ever have attacked him, and put them in a position to watch the fight.

They looked at each other, their hands shaking. The battle had taken them back to a world of no men, a world before men, when great beasts ruled the primitive distances of untouched land and fought each other for mastery.

Very slowly, they began working their way up through the stream growth.

Both the lion and the grizzly were dead. They were still locked together, piled in a shapeless mound on the ground. It looked as though all the bones in both their bodies were broken.

One of the miners cautiously prodded the lion with his toe, still half-expecting that formless mass to turn once more into the thing of deadliness and daring and beauty it had been in the battle.

They knelt and looked at the bodies more closely. The lion's fangs were locked deeply in the grizzly's cheek. His throat and back were ripped. The cat's hind legs had torn all the hide off his belly. Her feet were buried inside him.

The two miners walked back toward their claim and began figuring the best way to climb the cliff after the kittens.

XVI

AMERICAN LIONS AND TIGERS

IF more of the big-game hunters of this country adopted a See-America-First attitude, few of them would ever venture abroad and those that did would be extremely disappointed. For the two big cats of this continent, the puma and the jaguar, are more challenging to pursue and more dangerous to corner than any of their slightly larger relatives in far-off places.

It's becoming exceedingly difficult, these days, to be impressed with the trophies brought back by the globe-trotter.

Perhaps he displays, for the admiration of his friends, the long-maned pelt of an African lion. His white hunter warned him this was a dangerous undertaking, he mentions, but he went ahead, he went on into the unknown reaches of the Dark Continent, met the King of Beasts in his own territory and conquered him.

Maybe the striped hide of a tiger hangs on his wall. This one was a man-hunter, of course. A virtual reign of terror existed in that particular province of India until our friend showed up in the nick of time and succeeded where all others had failed.

Actually, the methods by which these two pieces of fur left the backs of their wearers and ended up on that trophy-room wall are a little less glamorous.

At the same time the American sportsman was getting off the boat at Nairobi, the company that had arranged his safari was busily training his lion to come and get itself killed. Each day, at a given time, a truck was driven out to a spot where a prize was known to be lying up and chunks of freshly-killed meat were unloaded. After a few blasts on the horn, the truck was driven off. By the time the hunter arrived, coming at the sound of the horn was a conditioned reflex in the doomed lion.

"Not sporting to shoot them lying down," the guide informed his client in a Hemingway voice, "I'll see if I can rouse them. If they charge, I'll back you up."

At the sound of the horn, the lions trotted eagerly toward the truck. The American hunter dropped the biggest male in his tracks, sincerely believing he was stopping a charging man-killer. The other lions turned and ran in surprise.

The Indian shikar is only slightly less commercialized than the African safari and what difference exists will disappear rapidly as more American hunters try the Far East. The most inoffensive tiger in all India becomes a man-hunter upon the arrival of a sportsman with American dollars in his pocket. High and safe in his *machan*, he somehow manages to keep on believing the creature he's hunting is a ferocious, deadly killer and that the local natives are living in fear of their lives. He never wonders why these same unarmed natives, for a small sum, accepted so eagerly the task of driving the tiger toward his stand.

Actually, among tigers, the man-hunter is an extremely rare exception. The great striped cats turn to stalking men only when they've grown too feeble and lost too many teeth to hunt their usual prey. The few man-hunters that crop up from time to time are hardly trophy specimens. And even if they were, they'd still be promptly dispatched by government authorities, not reserved for the tourist trade. The average Indian tiger lives out his life, sometimes in the very outskirts of cities and towns, without causing any alarm among the natives.

The American *tigre*, the jaguar, is not going to be killed from the safety of any tree platform. He's far too wary and far too dangerous. Even in a section where the jungle floor is littered with his tracks, the big spotted cat is so sly that a large pack of highly-skilled dogs must be used to run him down. This often takes many days, for the hunting range of a single jaguar may cover a wide territory. Once the dogs bring the big cat to bay, he usually retreats into a thicket to make his fight. If the hunter can arrive while he still has dogs left and get in a killing shot while the big cat's attention is being held, he has an even chance of winning his trophy in comparative safety.

Of course, the big-game hunter with Africa and India under his belt may very well scorn the thought of safety, actually seek danger in his love of excitement. In that case, he might well try the sport worked out by *tigreros*, such as Sascha Siemel, who has lectured on this subject extensively in the United States and now makes his home in Pennsylvania. When a jaguar is brought to bay by the dogs, the hunter advances on the cat with a long spear and attracts his attention just as though he were bull-fighting. When he gets too close, the maddened jaguar charges. The *tigrero* drops the butt of the spear to the ground and braces himself.

There are, of course, uncertainties to this sport. The American tiger may not leap at all, but charge low and attack on the ground. He may feint, dodge back, and slash in from the side. But the lack of such uncertainties would of course destroy the very purpose of this sport.

Hunting the American lion, the puma or cougar, may be a better adventure for the sportsman who wishes to get acquainted with New World big cats. The puma has been hunted so much that he has a deep awareness of man's ability to kill him, and he seldom fights back now, even when cornered. Instead of making his stand in a thicket, he usually climbs a tree and stays there while the dogs rage beneath him. A good man with a rifle is seldom in danger.

But there are exceptions. And this gives an added tang to lion hunting. Pumas *have* fought back when cornered, *have* attacked, killed and eaten men. A hunter may kill a dozen cats without getting a scratch. The next one may be the one whose anger conquers its fear.

Recently, a movie short was filmed that portrayed a new sport invented by Western puma-hunters. Leaving their rifles at home, they rode hard after their hounds until a lion had been treed. Without fear of attack, they climbed up within a few feet of the big cat and slipped a noose around his neck. After yanking him down to the ground, one of the hunters further amused himself by grabbing the lion's tail and swinging him around in circles. Then the puma was tied securely and brought back alive.

At the same time that theaters all over this country were showing that film, a new outbreak of puma attacks was taking place on Vancouver Island. One young boy had been killed. More than a dozen people had been pounced upon and horribly mauled without provocation.

This is the American lion. He's a cat with a tawny hide, steel muscles, oversized fangs and claws and a split personality. He's a skulking coward, too chilled with fear to defend himself. At the same time he's a skillful murderer, a deadly man-killer.

All in all, he's a far more mysterious and unfathomable cat than any prowling the jungles of Africa and India.

It should also be mentioned that a good many men whose trophy rooms boast big-cat hides from the other side of the world would drop dead from exhaustion attempting to stay with the hounds on a puma chase. When the trail leaves the low country and heads up the sierra toward the peaks, you'll go first through timberland, fallen logs and blowdowns. Then you'll ride into tight, thick scrub that whips your horse and does as expert a job on your hide as the cat you're hunting might. If you make it and get above the timber line, you'll find great open gorges, tight ledges, loose rock and belly-deep snow for your horse to flounder in. Then, as likely as not, the cat will take you back down, then up again. It won't be any suburban bridle path.

However, if you insist on forgoing the comforts of Africa and hunting an American lion, good guides with experienced hound packs are ready to take you. Pumas are still abundant in numbers sufficient for hunting in a few Western areas. A letter to the State Tourist Bureau, Santa Fe, New Mexico; Development Board, Arizona State Building, Phoenix, Arizona; or Tourist and Publicity Council, 210 State Capitol Building, Salt Lake City, Utah, will give you the names of guides and lodges and all other information needed to plan your trip.

Hunting the American tiger will be a little more difficult. The biggest jaguars live in the jungles of Southern Brazil. Getting there is extremely expensive, more so than going abroad, since commercial hunting in the African sense does not yet exist. There may be jaguars within the boundaries of the United States today, but finding one of them would be a near-impossibility. You'd best try for the big spotted cat on his Mexican range. Several good guides advertise regularly in American outdoor magazines. Take time and care in selecting one, ask for references and demand a detailed outlining of expenses.

In Mexico's jungle, you'll probably hunt from a boat at night with a flashlight, since the rivers are the only paths through this cover. In the mountains, hounds may be used or you may keep watch in the cover beside a waterhole.

With hard work and a great deal of luck, you may obtain a rare trophy. The pelt of the jaguar, perhaps the most beautiful of any furred creature in existence, is usually bright yellow and patterned with large black spotted rosettes. The base color may vary from clear gold to a tawny shade; the spots, from jet black to brownish black. There have been albino jaguars. There is also a black or melanistic color phase, a rare animal whose spots are lost in the dark shade of his fur. It is popularly believed that black jaguars are more fierce and deadly than others.

The hide of the American lion is most often colored reddish brown, with dark ears and a dark tip on his tail, a white belly and white on the upper parts of his hind legs. The shading of the main color may vary slightly with the season. Blue-gray or slate-colored pumas have been killed in the United States, but they are extremely rare. In the tropics, both albino pumas and jet-black pumas are found, but they do not exist on the northern range.

The puma has the widest distribution of any New World mammal, from the northernmost sections of British Columbia to the Magellan Straits area in Argentina. Before the coming of white men to this continent, these cats were abundant from ocean to ocean.

The range of the jaguar has always been more restricted. A few have migrated as far south as Argentina and as far north as the Grand Canyon, but most of these cats live in dense remote sections of South and Central American jungles.

The heaviest jaguar on record weighed 280 pounds, but there is every reason to believe the largest of the American tigers sometimes scale well over 300. The record books will tell you that the biggest puma was the 227-pound cat that Theodore Roosevelt killed in Colorado in 1901. This is carrying presidential immunity too far. A lion that weighed 276 pounds after the intestines had been removed was shot near Hillside, Arizona, in 1917 by a government hunter named J. R. Patterson. This is a freak size. An average full-grown puma will weigh 150 pounds; a jaguar, 180.

The largest lions are usually taken at the extreme northern and southern ends of the range. In the tropics, they are much smaller. The size of jaguars is not determined by the range.

Both the puma and the jaguar were worshipped as gods by the early Indians in most parts of the Americas. Although only one puma shrine is known to have existed in the United States, in Sandoval County, New Mexico, it's certain that many American tribes considered the big cats to be sacred.

Most of the tribes that were conquered by the Incas, at the time when their empire extended nearly 3000 miles, were cat-worshippers. But the Incas themselves were not. They hunted pumas and jaguars for sport, kept them as pets and used them to kill prisoners in arenas that were remarkably similar to the amphitheatres of the Romans.

In Argentina, a modified form of puma-worship still exists among the plainsmen, who call this big cat The Friend of Man, even though he may feed off their sheep regularly. Legend, or perhaps history, has it that in 1536 the people of Buenos Aires were under siege by the Indians. 1800 of the town's 2000 inhabitants died of starvation and their bodies were merely thrown outside the walls of the fort-like city. Wild beasts by the thousands came out of the jungle to feed.

A young girl named Maldonada was captured by the Indians. Some time later, when peace had been made, she was returned with other prisoners, but the people of Buenos Aires falsely accused her of treason and condemned her to death. She was tied to a tree in the midst of the corpses, and left to the mercy of the wild.

Two nights passed before soldiers went out to bring in her bones. They found her unharmed. A puma had come to her side, she insisted, and guarded her throughout the entire time of her ordeal, fighting bravely to defend her against the jaguars and other wild creatures who attacked. It had ended its vigil only when it heard the soldiers coming.

American lions and tigers are remarkably similar in most characteristics. Their mating habits are much alike. The mother cats breed once every two years. Several males may meet and fight for the privilege of being first, but the female usually accommodates the losers also. The gestation period is about one hundred days. Whelping time may be any season of the year, although there is a slight tendency in the colder extremes of the range for kittens to arrive most often in spring.

The male cat seldom remains with the female after the breeding. One exceptional male puma, some years back in Colorado, stayed with his mate until the kittens were a month old. The female was killed at this time and the male went back to the den and ate the kittens. He returned several times after that, still looking for his mate. One day he found a hunter and a pack of hounds waiting for him. A terrific battle followed and he killed a dog before escaping.

Three is the average litter for a puma, two for a jaguar, although there may be any number from one to six. Puma kittens do not resemble the parents. They have spots and rings on their tails. Jaguar kittens are more brownish than adults and have spots rather than rosettes. Kittens of both species mature slowly. Their mothers spend nearly two years teaching them how to hunt before leaving to mate again. The young cats seldom breed until they are three years old.

An American lion may live as long as eighteen years. The longevity of the American tiger is probably slightly greater. Both of these cats, when they reach an old age, have trouble stalking and killing their usual prey. This may cause them to turn to livestock. It may even make man-hunters out of them.

Pumas and jaguars are slightly smaller than their relatives across the oceans, but their strength is every bit as great. A puma once killed a large calf, carried it over a four-foot-high fence and up a rock-strewn cliff where one measured leap with his load was fifteen feet. Another dragged a six-hundred pound heifer half-way up a mountainside. The strength of the jaguar is greater in proportion to its size. Both species can leap farther, attack more rapidly and are faster in general than the larger African or Indian cats.

American lions and tigers may travel as much as thirty miles in a single night merely from wanderlust. If hunting conditions become poor, they may migrate even farther. Some years ago actor Clark Gable was puma hunting, ably guided by government hunter Charles Vaughan. A four-month-old cat was treed by the hounds and Gable took it alive, intending to make a pet of it. He put a dog collar on it, named it "Rowdy" and engraved this on the collar plate. Rowdy escaped the first night and the hounds refused to hunt the same lion twice. A year later Vaughan captured this cat seventy-five miles away with its collar and nameplate still intact.

Neither New World cat attempts to run down its dinner as a wolf, for instance, does. Both depend on slow, careful stalking, then a sudden, bounding charge. The lion usually strikes by springing as much as thirty feet and then smashing down on his prey with both forepaws, a blow that can snap the neck of a full-grown elk very easily. The jaguar may leap or charge in a straight run like a bear.

Pumas and jaguars alike are extremely silent animals, so much so that some naturalists have insisted they are mute. Actually, both are capable of making a wide variety of noises. The most common cry of the jaguar is a deep, throaty grunt. Sometimes he goes through the jungle talking to himself. The voice of the puma is much higher pitched. At mating time and when fighting, he may scream. Pioneer journals invariably describe this cry as similar to that of a woman being tortured. More modern accounts say that it's much like magnifying the yowling of a backyard tomcat many times. Lions can also mew, growl and hiss.

An extreme playfulness has been noticed to be a trait of American big cats when left undisturbed in their own environment. They cavort and gambol like small kittens. An honest and respected naturalist once checked and accepted as true a story of a full-grown jaguar who attempted to join two small Indian children at play. The children were fascinated and too young to know fear. But after a few minutes the big cat accidentally scratched the younger one, who began to cry. His brother picked up a stick and struck the jaguar, who turned and ran off into the jungle.

Other than man, American lions and tigers have few enemies in their various ranges against which they cannot successfully defend themselves. They may meet each other where their hunting ranges overlap and fight bitterly. Because of his superior speed and agility, the puma usually wins these battles in spite of the greater strength and size of his opponent. However, there are no pumas in the regions where the largest jaguars live.

If captured as kittens, pumas make fascinating pets and are usually very tame and affectionate. When full-grown they often have to be disposed of, not because of danger to man, but because they instinctively kill dogs and other domestic animals. A female puma was once trained to draw a small cart down the streets of a village in Montana.

The jaguar, as a pet, is highly dangerous and unreliable. Few animal trainers attempt to include them in their shows. They are more difficult and treacherous than leopards.

The American lion has a habit of following men for long distances, perhaps merely from curiosity, perhaps for more sinister reasons. This trait has not been noticed in the American tiger. But there is no doubt that both these creatures, on very rare occasions, have attacked and killed human beings without provocation.

XVII

CATS THAT HUNT MEN

On December 17, 1924, a small group of hunters walked down a shadowy canyon in Okanogan County, Washington. They were not sportsmen hunting for pleasure and flushed with excitement at the beginning of a day's chase. They walked in grim silence and studied the snow. There in the whiteness a story could be read from foot-prints, scuff-marks and blood-stains.

On the day before, at eleven in the morning, a thirteen-year-old boy named Jimmy Fehlhaber had started out to borrow a team of horses from a neighboring ranch. The mercury was shrinking back into the bulb of the thermometer and Jimmy walked briskly along, even ran a few steps as he went down the slope of the canyon, but nothing in the spacing of his tracks indicated he had any warning of danger.

From the underbrush at the canyon's edge, the eyes of a hunting puma watched his approach. It came to the edge of the cover at a shambling walk. Suddenly it backed up one step, then flattened in the brush. It was without motion now, except for the heaving of the furred flanks. It watched the boy with gooseberry-colored eyes.

Jimmy Fehlhaber was not carrying a rifle. Had he been armed the outcome would most likely have been the same. He was still not aware of the big cat as it hurried across the clearing and crouched at the base of a large pine.

One tremendous bound carried the puma twenty-nine feet

through the air. It landed on Jimmy's shoulders, smashed him to the snow and then dug in with fang and claw.

But the boy did not give in to death quickly and easily. With the courage of desperation he fought the big killer cat for several minutes. His hat and mittens came off in this battle. He managed to get his pocket knife out and opened. But he was very seriously wounded. Part of his scalp and a piece of bone from his skull were later found at this spot.

Somehow, Jimmy found the strength to fight his way back to his feet. He tried to run, stumbled and staggered more than forty feet, most of the time dragging the full weight of the puma as it sunk its fangs into his neck, then ripped and tore at his legs and sides with all four feet. The teeth of the lion broke the arteries. Blood spurted out to drench the snow. This was the death blow.

Still, the boy found the incredible strength to go on another dozen steps and climb into the lower branches of a tree. This was a hopeless attempt, for the puma is a very capable climber. But, in the fading consciousness of the boy as his life drained away, this effort was a symbol of fighting to the end, never giving up.

Most likely Jimmy was already dead when the lion pulled him down. There was no further sign of struggling.

The puma dragged the boy to a dense growth of brush a hundred yards away. There, in seclusion, it fed on the body.

This may seem a normal enough thing for a mountain lion who has just killed a human to do. But the cases where it has happened, throughout the entire reach of American natural history, may be counted on the fingers of one hand.

The government hunters who followed the tracks of the big cat up the mountainside that day in 1924 knew this. They also knew something that made their hunting a matter not a revenge but of urgent necessity. Once a lion successfully attacks a human being he is likely to hunt man again.

The trail of the killer led up the mountain to an overhanging cliff that gave protection from the icy wind and a view of the death site. The puma had waited several hours here and would have returned to feed again if the boy's body had remained undiscovered. Because of the disturbance below, it had gone on into the mountains and its trail faded out on the hardened crust. When darkness came, with an eighteen-below-zero wind shrieking through the peaks, the hunters gave up for the night.

Citizens throughout the entire state, shocked into action, donated large sums as rewards for the killer cat. These funds were increased by the county treasury until nearly everyone who owned a rifle throughout the Okanogan Mountains became a puma hunter. The bloated bounties were paid out on a dozen big cats brought in. Although it is safe to assume the real killer cat met his end shortly after Jimmy's death, to this day there is some dispute about which was the guilty lion.

The most likely suspect seemed to be a three-year-old cat that a local rancher found in his coyote trap on January 20. The stomach of this puma contained a small undigested mass which proved to be human hair and cloth from blue jeans. The Biological Survey laboratories backed up the opinion that this was the killer cat.

But a great many men were unconvinced, among them the government hunters who had been working constantly since Jimmy's death and who kept on working after the trapped cat had been brought in and publicized. These men pointed out that killer pumas were invariably much older than three years. A claw had been found at the murder scene and the big cat's track had been tinted with red. No claw was missing from the trapped lion. Doubt was expressed that hair and cloth could hold out against a puma's powerful digestive juices for five weeks. The accusation that someone had shoved cloth and hair down a young lion's throat to get the reward was publicly flung.

Another likely suspect and one that satisfied the professional hunters was killed near Winthrop a little later. A blacksmith, George Vanderpool, heard children screaming. With the Fehlhaber boy's death fresh in his mind he grabbed a rifle and ran over. Three children on their way home from school had been stalked by a large puma, but their screams had frightened it off.

Vanderpool owned a few good lion-hunting dogs; the lion was soon treed and the blacksmith's aim was good. This cat was an older female, as most killer cats are. When she proved to have a claw missing identical to the one found at the death scene, even the skeptical government hunters believed that Jimmy Fehlhaber's murderer no longer prowled the Okanogan Mountains.

For almost another year various rewards were paid for pumas brought in. But it's fairly certain that the man-hunting cat was one of these two. Most wildlife experts who examined the case believe it was the three-year-old. The predator-hunters insist the Winthrop lion was the one. The mystery will never be solved.

On the average of about once a year, someone in this country is reported to have been attacked by a puma. Most such attacks are the result of a frightened person's imagination, not the puma's aggressiveness. And of the cases that are authentic, only a small percentage could be called unprovoked. The great majority of the actual attacks do not result in serious injury, and anyone who examines vital statistics will see just how extreme a rarity a death from puma-attack is. Jimmy Fehlhaber's death is the only recorded case in this century where a puma has fed on human flesh.

A puma attack is like a puma scream. Both are so infrequent that many men have insisted they simply do not exist.

Several outdoorsmen, who hunted the big cat year after year without hearing a scream, have insisted in their notes that a puma is a mute animal and that the stories of its screams result from a combination of human imagination and the sounds made by great horned owls. These men had me believing they were right until a caged female puma let loose a shriek one day just a few feet from my eardrums.

The American lion is usually a timid cat. So respectful of humanity have most pumas been that naturalists have often insisted that all killer cats were products of human imagination. But Jimmy Fehlhaber's death was startling and convincing.

Pumas are characteristically wary, fearful and puzzled in their contacts with man. But there have been bold exceptions. One big cat crossed an inlet to set up his own hunting preserve in the deer paddock of the zoo in Stanley Park, Vancouver. The deer population of the zoo was steadily dropping until a pack of lion-hunting dogs were brought in.

Another bold Vancouver puma made the headlines about forty years ago. But there was far less humor in the story. Perhaps what made the headlines was the unbelievable courage of two young children.

Doreen Ashburnham was eleven. Anthony Farrer was eight. They lived on neighboring farms near the little town of Cowichan Lake. One September morning they set out to bridle and bring in their ponies from a meadow pasture.

The timber had been cleared from a great deal of this area but the land had not yet been turned by a plow. High grass and fern clumps had been left for pasture and it was through this cover that the two children moved on their way to the meadow.

The ferns had been touched by early frosts and taken on a red-brown color. Not twenty feet from the path the children were taking a puma lay in cover, its tawny shape invisible in the brown grasses. Light, silent and cautious was its every move. It drifted like a tendril of fog toward the children, then crouched with its head between its extended forepaws and the end of its tail waving slightly.

The children knew little of natural checks and balances. They did not realize that a change had taken place on Vancouver Island in the last few decades and that this change would be reflected in the characters of the big cats that nightly prowled those northwest forests. Once, in this land, there had been only the wild things and they had prospered or dwindled together, balanced in natural law. But then lumbering men had come to level great stretches of the forests. Second-growth is far better deer browse than virgin spruce timber. As the trees grew back the deer herd multiplied. Accordingly the number of big cats increased also. But homesteaders and farmers came quickly to settle in the wake of the lumbering men. These men hunted deer—hunted them for food, hunted them to protect crops. The herd dwindled. Predators began starving. There were too many of them now and too few deer.

The children were not thinking of these things that September morning. Nor was the puma. It most likely thought only of the terrible living pain hunger had become. It waited until the children had passed.

Then it burst suddenly from the cover and leaped on the eleven-year-old girl from behind. Doreen went sprawling to the ground and lay there, face down, held beneath the puma's claws as it prepared to feed.

The eight-year-old boy turned and saw this. Every nerve and muscle of his body must have writhed with fear, every instinct must have told him to escape. What he did instead I seriously doubt that very many grown men would have done. He yelled at Doreen to lie still. Then he leaped directly upon the puma's back, wrapping his arms around its neck and wrestling it away from the fallen girl. She staggered back to her feet.

The big cat finally threw Anthony from its back, then struck hard at the boy's head. Claws ripped through his cheek and flipped him back to the ground. Instantly the puma pounced on him to finish him off. Even then, Anthony kept shouting to Doreen to run, to get away while she could.

But the girl had no intention of leaving him. Just as the cat's fangs were closing on his head she attacked, whipping it desperately in the face with her bridle. When the cat turned on her she drew up every bit of her courage and shoved her bare fist into the puma's deadly-fanged mouth. She kept on smashing at it with her bridle.

It was at this moment that the cat decided there had to be easier prey somewhere than these two plucky kids. As suddenly as it had come, it turned and disappeared in the cover.

Both of the children were badly cut and bleeding heavily, but they recovered. The story brought a great deal of interest when it broke in the city newspapers. The government officials in the

Department of the Secretary of State of Canada made
speeches when they awarded the two children the Albe
of the Second Class for bravery. The men of Cowich
said little, acted quickly. Within a few hours the hou
neighbor, Charles March, had run that trail to its end
human-hunting cat was a mere trophy.

It was an old female, so thin and starved that altho
measured seven feet nine inches long she weighed only
five pounds. She was very nearly blind and the possibili
that she may have mistaken the children for her usual p1

Although killings by puma occur occasionally in the s
part of the New World, just as they do here, they are
common than jaguar attacks. *El tigre*, the Spanish cal
biggest cat of the Americas, and he is the equal of the
tiger in almost every respect.

The ruins of what was once the Convent of San F
can still be seen today. They lie on the banks of the Rio
near a place called Pena Blanca, about eighteen mile
Santa Fe. Not too much more than a century ago, the C
was a place of many people and much activity with severa
ings and a large garden; a community within itself.

In the spring of 1825, the river flooded its banks an
pletely covered the densely-wooded off-shore islands,
the wildlife to seek higher ground.

On April 10, a lay brother dutifully made his confessic
went through his prayers. Then he started into the sacris
suddenly froze in terror. A giant jaguar lay crouched to
on the floor a few feet away.

The man had no time to reason that the great cat had ju
the garden wall and that a door to the sacristy had accide
been left open. Probably he did not even have time to co
plate on whether his prayers and confessions had been hi
efforts. The big cat was on him instantly, ripping and teari
him as it smashed him to the floor, then dragging him
corner and finishing him off.

The guardian of the convent was nearby and heard the screams. He dashed into the sacristy. Almost before he could realize what had happened the jaguar was on him. His shrieks of pain ended as suddenly as the first man's cries. A group of people were at the door now, still more puzzled and curious than afraid. They pushed inside, jamming tightly against each other in the narrow passageway. The big cat picked his third victim and killed him quickly and effortlessly.

Other convent people had started in through an adjoining back room. The jaguar bounded back to face this new danger from the rear. One man couldn't quite get back through the door in time. The others, running for the church now, heard his cries of "Save me!", heard them drowned out by the savage roars of the cat. They hid in the church. The jaguar slipped back to wait in the sacristy.

After some time, one of the men found the courage to slip over and bolt the doors, locking the cat in. Fearfully the crowd approached. Finally someone thought of boring a hole in the door.

A rifle was slipped through this hole and the shooting started. Even after the jaguar lay still, a great deal of ammunition was blasted into his body before anyone dared unbolt the door. Four men and a great yellow-and-black cat lay in blood that filled the sacristy like a garden pool.

Massacres as vicious as the one in the mission at San Francisco have always been unusual. But jaguar and puma killings were an accepted hazard of frontier life, in the early days of this country. Regional histories from nearly all sections of the big cats' range mention these attacks. The tombstone of Philip Tanner, in Lewisville, Pennsylvania, has a crude likeness of the cat that killed him engraved upon it.

When the continent was largely an unbroken stretch of wilderness the big cats probably hunted men almost as often as men hunted cats, especially when the deer herds began dwindling. In certain untouched areas this condition still prevails. Until

224

very recent years, the pumas of the Lake Viedma region of Argentina seemed to have no fear of men. The jaguars in many parts of the steaming mystery of the Matto Grasso are persistent man-hunters.

But throughout the greatest part of the range of the big cats, the advent of smokeless powder and flat-trajectory rifles has instilled a deep biting fear of man that rules their lives. The man-hunting cat of today is an exception and a rare one. It is usually an old female, her teeth and claws so worn that she is slowly dying of starvation. It may be a younger cat inflicted with rabies. It may merely be an unbalanced and unusually mean male, thrilling in destruction.

The individual variation among wild animals is as great as among humans. A killer cat of any species is as rare, as unfathomable and as dangerous as a criminally insane murderer among men.

XVIII

THE QUESTION OF SURVIVAL

SOMEWHERE in the West, a great tawny cat climbs out of a
hiding place in the rocks and makes his way along a ledge, far
from human eye. Night is coming on fast and the shadows of
the canyons are tinted with purple as they darken. The huge
cat's eyes are intent and unblinking. His head swings slowly
from side to side. His tail waves up and down but never quite
touches the rock. His nose wrinkles as he tests the night air
for scent. When this wild hunter nears his prey his movements
will become imperceptible. His crouched, muscular body will
drift as silently as a wisp of smoke.

The American lion is what biologists call a "highly successful

226

predator species." In the wild world, where only the strongest or fastest or best-armed creatures may survive, he has his place. In the world he knows, he reigns supreme.

But in the same steady, inexorable manner that he moves toward his prey, civilization is stalking him.

The question of survival does not concern the jaguar as yet. The American tiger was never common in this country. The bounties offered by the early Spanish authorities exterminated any that might be called native well over a century ago. Migrant jaguars from the Mexican range are all that may be expected in the future.

Throughout large sections of South and Central America, jaguars and pumas alike are still relatively numerous. It is highly improbable that the threat of extinction will arise within the next fifty years.

Within the boundaries of the United States, however, the future of the one remaining big cat, the puma, is extremely doubtful.

The range of the American lion once included every state in this country. Today, there is an even chance that pumas still exist in the wildest glades of Florida. There is a possibility, although extremely remote, that a few may still be holding out in Shenandoah National Park, in the river-bottom growth of Northern Louisiana or in the great forests of Northern Wisconsin or Michigan. More than likely, however, these cats will be found only in the Rocky Mountain states, the desert ranges of Arizona, Texas and New Mexico and in the coastal mountains of California, Oregon and Washington.

The American lion has been a hunted outlaw with a price on his head for four hundred years. Even before the Pilgrims landed, the Jesuit priests of California were offering the Indians a bounty of a bull for each puma killed. The early colonies began offering puma bounties soon after the first wolf bounties went into effect and the system spread westward in the same manner. Bounties were fraudulently claimed more often than not and never produced the desired results. But, somehow, they still exist.

Like all large predators, the lion population was reduced far more by civilization's destruction of suitable food supply and range than by actual hunting and trapping. But, even so, a ruthless campaign against the puma was fought on the livestock lands of this country. Poisoning was far more widespread than is generally admitted today, in spite of the federal government's opposition to its use. Hound packs and steel traps were the most common weapons and the most effective. The American lion was not as wise in the way of traplines as the stockmen's other principal enemy, the gray wolf.

Whether or not the war of extermination waged against the puma was justified is extremely doubtful. The big cats usually prefer their own remote mountain habitat to open pasture. Domestic stock has seldom been a major part of their diet.

A five-year study was made from 1918 through 1922 of the stomach contents of all lions killed throughout the western United States by government predator-control men. The following averages were determined: deer—60.4%, porcupines—19.5%, all types of livestock combined—11.5%, other wild creatures, carrion and grass—8.6%. Actually, the percentage of livestock kill is far higher than average here, due to the fact that the government hunters were invariably working on or near cattle ranges. In Colorado, Idaho, Montana, Oregon and Washington, no traces of domestic animals were discovered in puma stomachs. From the standpoint of protecting livestock, it is obvious that lion-control was far more widespread than was necessary.

Justified or not, the intense destruction of the American lion by the cattle-raising industry is virtually over and done with now. The amount of cattle killed by the puma in this country today is negligible. Most of the lion control that goes on now and most of the bounty systems still in effect exist supposedly to protect the herds of whitetail and mule deer.

The results of this philosophy in action are difficult to analyze. An extensive puma-extermination program that was put into

228

effect in the Upper Gila River Basin of New Mexico showed only one definite result—a fantastic increase in the number of coyotes. In other areas the destruction of these deer-killing cats has caused the whitetail herds to grow far too large for the browse. When this happens the deer become stunted and sickly and the winter toll soon reaches a level far above the previous lion kill. In all cases, puma extermination means a vast increase in the number of porcupines, since these creatures have few other enemies. The extent of the damage this causes to valuable timber cannot even be estimated.

How many deer does an average full-grown puma kill in a year? A few self-styled authorities have claimed three hundred. The biologists of the U. S. Fish and Wildlife Service give the figure as fifty or more. The most careful studies seem to indicate that it is a rare puma that kills more than thirty-five deer in any one year. One naturalist made a detailed examination of eleven puma-killed deer in New Mexico and discovered the surprising fact that every one of these animals was either diseased or abnormal. He found hoof deformities that slowed the whitetails down, pre-natal injuries that made them clumsy and awkward. He found heavy infestations of ticks and malproportions of leg bones and body length. What he failed to find was a single case of a normal healthy deer having been killed by a puma. Since it has been estimated that two out of three deer escape the attack of a lion, there can be little doubt that this cat is a prime factor in keeping deer herds at a vigorous healthy level by weeding out subnormal and sickly specimens.

Let's face it. The Power that created the puma knew what He was doing.

There is only the most remote possibility that the American lion will exist, outside of zoos and museums, within the borders of the United States fifty years from today.

Saving this fascinating and magnificent creature in his own environment will mean, first of all, saving that environment. This entails, in an immediate sense, defeating the efforts in Congress to turn our national forests into private pastures. These attempts are made by a small but powerful minority within the livestock industry and they are made regularly each year, usually hidden in some worthwhile piece of legislation. The history of national forest management should have made it clear by now that leasing grazing rights simply does not work out.

The chances of saving puma habitat in this country are doubtful. And this alone would not be enough to preserve the species for future generations of American hunters. The big cats need a protected mating season and freedom from bounties. Good lion country on which all lions have been exterminated exists in many states.

Michigan, for example, needs predation on the deer herd very badly. In the Lower Peninsula, there is practically none. Stunted deer, over-browsed cover and an unbelievably high starvation toll are the rule, not the exception. In the Upper Peninsula, the only force for keeping the deer herd in balance is a pitifully small handful of wolves who have held out for the last half-century in spite of the fact that bounties are offered for their hides. They cannot hold out much longer without protection. A new bridge is going across the Straits of Mackinac. Each time the big cranes fasten a new beam into place, the end draws a little nearer for one of the last refuges of wolves in this country.

There are far more whitetail deer in Michigan today than there were before the first white man set foot in the New World. The only areas where they are not starving are those regions where they feed on farm crops, causing far greater losses to man than wolves and lions combined ever did in the years when they were common. The Michigan Conservation Department, one of the best in the country, is too badly hamstrung by the State Legislature to even begin correcting the situation. The bounty laws remain on the books.

There are two basic, insurmountable fallacies to the very theory of predator control and the first is this—man will not and cannot take the place of a predator species. He is too well equipped for killing to restrict his destruction to deformed or diseased animals. His interest is in trophy specimens or healthy meat animals, usually the very creatures which should not be eliminated. A lion or a wolf, of course, is trying only to feed and stay alive. But Nature controls his predation and makes it a selective and beneficial process.

The second great weakness in any system of predator control is the inability of men to discard methods, habits and theories when they are worn out. The wild world itself changes constantly and rapidly. One species dwindles, another flourishes—just as though Nature had flipped a switch. But the values and practices of men progress slowly in comparison. Our present policy in regard to the American lion has not changed since the days when the West was first made safe for cattle.

The blame for the imminent extinction of the big cats will not rest solely with the cattle raisers. There is too much truth in the old saying about the fiddler-payer calling the tune. At the present time, the average citizen is footing the bill for protecting the livestock industry from foreign competition and paying every cent of the cost of exterminating predators so that this subsidized industry may expand. As long as the average citizen is content to do this, the American lion will move on down that long trail blazed by the hooves of the bison. No force on earth can save him.

If the conversion of national forests into pasture could be stopped, the second step would be an end to all control of the puma except that provided by sportsmen who are hunting for trophy and pleasure reasons. A fall and early winter open season would be justified at the moment, although special permits would have to be issued to stockmen who could prove puma predation on their herds. Destroying the small percentage of lions who actually prey on livestock would not appreciably affect the puma population. However, the costs of hunting down raider lions should be borne by the complaining stock owner, not the public. For only in this manner can such control be kept at its truly necessary level.

In brief, the action that must be taken to save the American lion is the same action that was taken, much too late, to save the grizzly.

This program may sound practical to anyone without a grasp of the firm entrenchment of bounty and control systems. Actually, it is the wildest and most unreasonable dream a conservationist could have. Nothing short of a miracle could keep the American lion, or almost any other large predator, in existence in this country for another fifty years.

The cat that paces gracefully along a lonely ledge, high above the timber line, has no glimpse of this. He moves on through the world he knows, the world in which he has a purpose, and realizes only that his domain is dwindling rapidly. He goes his way on silent feet, hunting because he must eat to live and kill to eat—a thing of beauty but a thing doomed.

Nature, with its grim laws of survival, allowed him to prosper. Men have ruled he can no longer be.

CONCLUSION

THE LAWS OF NATURE

SOME years back there was a saying or slogan that was commonly used by the men who were insisting Alaska had too many wolves and bears, the men who were demanding more intensive predator control. It had many forms and wordings, but in general it went something like this:

"Nature is impressive and marvelous. But man is still more impressive, still more marvelous. God, of course, is most marvelous of all."

I've long accepted the fact that the forces who wish to convert all wilderness into pasture and farmland are never going to run out of novel approaches. I'll readily admit they have almost as much imagination as they do power, money or political influence. I'm willing to face the unpleasant prospect of their always having a few new tricks up their sleeves.

But do they have to make believe that God put them there?

Actually, our rapidly disappearing wilderness itself is far more convincing testimony to the existence of a higher Power than any aspect of that which replaces it. In the wild all living things have a reason for existence, a vital place in a scheme of things that portrays the wisdom of the Creation more obviously and incontrovertibly than anything man could write or build or do. Just as this spinning earth is part of a delicately-balanced system of stars and planets and gravitational pulls and centrifugal forces, each particle of wilderness life, from the simplest organisms to the highly-perfected creatures described in this book, is a part of an intricately-compensated system that is itself

233

governed by this world's position in and movement through the universe. And where the laws of Nature are concerned, man is the outlaw, the renegade, the alien.

Nature has been experimenting with mammals for more than 200 million years. Early in the Triassic Period new forms of life appeared with certain basic and vital differences from the reptilian things that dominated the world of that day—constant blood temperature, larger brains, more complex blood circulation and breathing equipment. These creatures multiplied, diversified and specialized. For each group of mammals that came into existence to feed on plant life, new races of flesh-eaters and carrion-eaters evolved.

The history of mammals may be roughly divided into two stages: 180 million years of numerical growth during which every size, shape and form of creature imaginable had its possibilities tested; then 20 million years of intense competition through which only a fraction of the species that had once existed survived. Very seldom were these survivors the largest specimens their particular kind had ever produced. The sabre-toothed tiger went the way of the tyrannosaurus, but the puma lived on. The solitary dire wolf drifted into extinction, but the pack-running timber or gray wolf prospered until his range was world-wide. The strictly carnivorous cave bear disappeared, but his less particular relatives still walk the earth. Rather than size, strength or even intelligence, the requisites for survival seem to be these:

Each successful species must have a place and a purpose in the world.

Each must be the most perfect form of life that can be evolved to fill that place.

Before civilization laid siege to North America, the chain of life, the interdependency of every living thing on every other living thing, was functioning smoothly. For each peculiarity in the wrinkled surface of this continent, each variation in elevation, moisture and climate, a plant-eating species best suited to the range has been adapted. Predators most capable of successfully hunting these creatures had been developed. Subsidized animals, carrion-eaters, were here to clean up their kills.

The vast and fantastically complex system of predator-prey relationships was never seriously molested by the Indians and Eskimos who were here before us. The original American had invented a few tools, but he wasn't quite as successful at keeping himself fed as the wolves and pumas were. Even with his spears and arrows, he was never a match in combat for the larger bears. But he had a place in the wild scheme of things. His weapons were primitive enough so that his hunting, his predator functions, served to clean up the least-fit members of any species on which he preyed. And he himself was held constantly in check by starvation, by disease, by inter-tribal warfare—the same biotic checks that kept the wolves from dominating this continent.

The three groups of animals described in this book were the major predators and all three ranged from ocean to ocean. The hunting grounds of the American lion included practically all land south of the timber line. Wolves were found on the very northernmost reaches of land. Some bears lived on the fringes of the Mexican jungle; others lived on the ice of the Arctic Ocean. But lesser wild hunters had also made a place for themselves.

In the dense thickets of the Rio Grande delta, little long-tailed cats called eyras preyed on the birds and rats and mice. In that same cover the larger ocelot also hunted, showing a special taste for snakes. Occasionally one of the great jaguars would wander up through that land, feeding mainly on peccaries, never quite able to extend its range as successfully as the puma had done.

The little bobcat, an effective instrument for controlling the cottontail rabbit, ranged from this cover north to present-day Southern Canada, slightly overlapping the hunting grounds of the tuft-eared, snowshoe-footed Canada lynx, an equally effective instrument for controlling the varying hare.

Many creatures, like coyotes and foxes and wolverines, served the functions of both predator and carrion-eater. On the plains the

235

coyotes and foxes followed the wolves to clean up the buffalo carcasses, but they also hunted for themselves, stalking jackrabbits and geese and rodents. On the Barrens the wolverines followed the wolves to get the scraps of the caribou kills, but this largest member of the weasel family also preyed on ground mice and lemmings.

Other weasels had their own secure place and purpose. The smallest were skillful hunters of rodents. The marten was a weasel who took to the trees to hunt squirrels and the mink was a weasel who took to the water to hunt muskrats, never however becoming as completely aquatic as the otter. A still larger weasel was the fisher, who never fished but hunted both in the trees and on the ground, able to prey on a wide variety of animals.

There were many more, of course. The predatory mammals varied from the tiny mouse-hunting shrew, milligram for milligram the most savage creature on earth, to the great killer whale who preyed on all the creatures of the sea and was preyed on by none. The chain of life was infinitely complex, especially in the tropics. Any attempt to outline, even briefly, the interdependency of all creatures on the North American continent would require many volumes.

Perhaps the best range to single out would be the Barrens, the tundra ground north of the spruces. At first glance, life still farther north on the ice-pack itself might appear to be simpler. But Arctic life is really pegged to the sea. And ocean life is more complex than even that of the tropics. The Barrens are far from barren. Enough varieties of predator, prey and intermediate species exist there to show the pattern that is basically the same in all regions.

Before the coming of white men the strongest single force affecting wilderness life was the changing of the seasons. And on the Barrens this response of all living things to the earth's circling around the sun was complete and obvious.

In spring the caribou left their scattered range in the upper fringes of the spruce forests and pushed out over the tundra with their new calves to feed on the mosses and lichens that were being bared by melting snow. The wolves could not follow immediately, for pups had been born and were lying blind and helpless in the dens. But previously, from mid-February to the end of March, the wolves had been slaughtering far more than they could eat and burying the surplus.

But there was another wild hunter to harass the caribou during the northward migration. The great Barrens grizzlies were coming out of hibernation now, hungry and determined. The bears could not run down caribou, but they made an occasional kill by careful stalking, a welcome feast after living on ground mice. Just as wolf predation served to develop the speed and stamina of the caribou, grizzly predation sharpened their wariness.

The greatest inroads made on these sub-Arctic deer during the spring trek came from the Inland Eskimos, the people to whom caribou were the only means of life. The Eskimos could kill caribou in the quantity they needed only at the times of migration, so their lives too were governed by the seasons.

Wolverines and white foxes dug ground squirrels and lemmings, stalked Arctic hares and waited for the wolves to come north and provide them with free meals of caribou. In the upper reaches of tundra the giant musk oxen grazed. Because of their yard-long hair they had no need to migrate. They also had little fear of wolves and grizzlies and Eskimos, for the oxen had earned their right to survive by developing an impregnable defense. When attacked they formed a tight circle with only lowered heads and sharp horns showing. Only lone animals that had wandered from the herd were ever pulled down by predators. And even then this northern equivalent of the African water buffalo usually managed to take a few of his tormentors with him.

When summer came the browse was rich on the Barrens. But the wolves had now come north with their pups and were teaching them how to hunt, at the same time keeping the caribou from overpopulating. Rabies, tapeworms, mange mites, interpack warfare and the inherent dangers in hunting creatures so much larger than themselves all served to keep the wolves from overpopulating and thus destroying not only the caribou, but also themselves and the carrion-eaters they subsidized. For now that the wolves had arrived, foxes and wolverines were giving up the idea of working for a living and were following the trails of these larger, more capable hunters. The wolves, incidentally, were never too happy about providing meals for other animals. They caught, killed and ate foxes at every opportunity. For some unknown reason, though, they observed a silent truce with the wolverine.

There was little room for waste in the wild before the coming of white men. Every aspect of existing life that might provide support for a new form of life had been explored. And if, occasionally, the carcass of a kill was overlooked to mold back into the earth, the plant life compensated by growing more lushly from enriched soil.

The summer air above the tundra was dark with clouds of blackflies and mosquitoes. Solid swarms of them lay in wait in the thickets of dwarf willows. But they too were a part of the system, a minute part that served two purposes. First, they helped to test the fitness for survival of the larger forms of life. These tiny insects could weaken a caribou enough to provide the difference between escaping wolves and falling prey to them. They could also weaken a wolf enough so that the meal he chased outran him. Second, it was on the larva of these insects that the baby shrews fed from the time of their weaning until they were old enough to kill lemmings.

And lemmings had to be killed. These tiny northern mice multiplied so rapidly that without predation they might have destroyed the tundra browse in one season. The shrews were the main hunters of lemmings, but the ermines fed on shrews and lemmings both. When wolf-killed caribou was not available, the white foxes fed on ermines, shrews and lemmings indiscriminately. When caribou themselves were not available, the wolves might feed on all of these creatures and white foxes too.

The lemmings lived in complex burrows, complete cities of underground tunnels. Year after year, their numbers would increase and the numbers of the creatures who preyed on them and the creatures who preyed on those creatures would increase correspondingly. Then suddenly a lemming migration would begin. Compelled by some concept or instinct or need men have not yet fathomed, these little plant-eaters would leave their cities and move out across the tundra in a solid carpet. The migration urge would spread until all the Barrens was alive with lemmings. Nothing could stop them as long as they lived. They scurried into wide rivers, great lakes, even the ocean itself and swam on until they either drowned or were eaten by fish. They coated earth and water alike with a layer of living flesh.

It was during a migration year that the danger of lemmings destroying the browse and therefore all creatures who ranged over it was the greatest. But Nature had provided for this in a very strange way. When the migration began, all other creatures, even the plant-eaters, discarded their normal habits and fed on lemmings. The caribou and musk oxen mashed them down with their hooves by the thousands, then swallowed their fill. These creatures did not, of course, realize that they were saving their normal food supply by suddenly becoming carnivora after many years of remaining strictly herbivorous. Most likely some accumulative deficiency in diet brought about the sudden change of taste. But this is just one more facet of Natural wisdom, one more fascinating bit of evidence that Nature is more capable of looking after Her own than the experimental gropings of men can ever be.

A small seed stock of lemmings always remained behind in the burrows and refused to migrate. The year that followed a migration year would show a sharp decrease, of course, in the numbers of shrews and ermines. Then the cycle would begin again.

In autumn the caribou started south for the spruces, marching in far larger herds than during the spring trek, moving like an endless river of solid flesh. And all along the migration routes they ran a gauntlet of death. The wolves came with them like collie dogs herding sheep. The Eskimos made their major hunt

239

at this time. The grizzlies took their toll too, building up a fat supply for the long winter sleep. Crippled and deformed animals were pulled down easily. Diseased or tick-laden caribou rarely lived to carry their imperfections into the spruces. Old sterile bulls, powerful but slow, were common prey. Only caribou that were swift and wary and healthy reached the forests.

Then winter closed down. A few snow-trapped caribou might remain on the Barrens. A few wolves might stay behind and attempt to get through the long months of darkness and cold by hunting the big Arctic hares. But in general, the foxes and wolverines had to hunt for themselves now, digging down through snow and frozen earth after the little rodents.

The grizzlies slept well in their dens if they'd fed well through the autumn, living off stored fat. Otherwise, hunger might force them out to hunt in mid-winter. If the fall caribou kill had been successful, the Eskimos also hibernated, secure in their snow lodges. And all of the permanent darkness, the incessant blizzard and the fifty-below cold couldn't destroy their religious trust in that which they expected of Nature—the return of spring and the return of the caribou.

Did the Eskimo realize, as he swatted mosquitoes from his face, that his very existence depended on these devilish little insects? Did he understand that without mosquitoes there would be no shrews, that without shrews there would be too many lemmings, that with too many lemmings there would be no caribou? Of course not. No more so than the wolf who returned in rage to find his kill molested realized that the fox who robbed him played a vital part in keeping the caribou herds well fed by digging lemmings in the winter. No more so than the old bull caribou who went down under the slashing fangs of wolves realized that his death would increase the herd by giving the cows he'd guarded a chance to bring forth calves once more.

There was order and there was meaning in all things that lived and died on the wild land. There was little need for understanding.

*　　*　　*

240

When white men first penetrated the North American continent, they discovered the greatest teeming reservoir of wildlife that had been known throughout all recorded history. On the central plains alone, the buffalo and antelope and elk numbered more than one hundred million. It seemed impossible that a land so rich in game resources could ever be seriously depleted. The wild things had been there forever and would be there forever, the early white men believed.

From the time when we first settled the eastern seaboard we paid bounties for the destruction of wolves and pumas, just as the Spanish had been doing for some time in the Mexican provinces. But the early waste of game animals was minute and gradual, just as the early attempts at predator-extermination were ineffective. By 1800, wildlife had been destroyed only in the few small areas where the wilderness had been destroyed.

Then the beaver trappers went West. By 1840 beavers were too few to be profitable and the trappers turned to buffalo hunting. Next came the professional wolfer, who brought in his hides by shooting buffalo, poisoning the carcasses, then returning a few days later to skin out the dead wolves and coyotes and foxes. Then cattle came to the plains and the long bitter war between wolves and cattlemen began. (Few men, incidentally, realize just how close the wolves came to winning this war.)

Most of the wasteful destruction of game resources took place during the three short decades from 1850 to 1880, one mere generation of human time. At the beginning of this period, the game herds on the plains seemed inexhaustible. At the end of this time, only a few scattered pockets remained.

The beginning of the twentieth century was a turning point in some ways. Conservation came into being. An angry public demanded that a little of wild America be preserved. As far as the creatures described in this book are concerned, only the bears benefited in any way from the advent of conservation. The wolves and the big cats became convenient scapegoats to be blamed for the damage men had done.

I have no quarrel, once again, with those who insist that civilization and the larger wild mammals cannot exist in close proximity. As wasteful as the slaughter of the vast game herds that roamed the plains seems to have been, that region is at least being used productively by men today.

But we are making little use of the greatest share of both the mountain ranges and the northern spruce forests. We are making no use whatsoever of the Barrens. On that bleak treeless wasteland our apparent determination to eliminate all other major carnivora from the face of this continent stands out in all of its senselessness and inconsistency.

The predator-prey relationships that existed on the tundra before the coming of white men have been outlined briefly. That system, remember, had been working successfully for thousands of years. Caribou and wolves and Eskimos alike had found a place for themselves, a means of survival. No one of these three threatened either of the others with extinction. Eskimos doubtlessly faced an occasional starving winter, as did wolves and caribou. But in general these primitive people were better fed before they made the acquaintance of a higher civilization than they are today.

On the Alaskan tundra the greatest single blow that was dealt to the caribou economy was the importation of reindeer. Whether these European cousins of the caribou were brought here to provide a permanent food supply for the Eskimos, as is usually claimed, or whether the reasons for this importation were a little less humanitarian and a little more commercial would be a good topic for a debate. The reindeer prospered at first. A herd that at one time topped a million came from the original 1,280 transplanted animals. In fact, reindeer meat was soon being shipped down to the States and sold at a price with which the politically-entrenched cattle industry didn't care to compete. One point cannot be debated—it was a desire to keep reindeer meat off the market, not a desire to help the Eskimos, that caused the Reindeer Act to be passed. This piece of legislation made it illegal for white men to herd or sell reindeer.

The American Eskimos have always been hunters, never

herdsmen like the Laplanders. They made no attempt to herd reindeer. Instead, they let them run wild and hunted them exactly as they hunted caribou. Centuries of domesticity had of course rendered these creatures helpless against wolf predation. And as they interbred with native caribou, this helplessness was passed on like a plague.

Actually, of course, the caribou herds had been doomed from the time when modern rifles were first placed in the hands of the Eskimos. For a few short wonderful years they fed themselves and clothed themselves as they never had before. Often, on a fall migration, they killed so many that they ate nothing but the tongues. Then, very suddenly, there weren't enough caribou left to support them, rifles or no rifles. Many of the Inland Eskimos moved down to join the Coastal Eskimos, learning to take their food from the sea or else begging for the scraps thrown them by white men at places like Point Barrow. Puzzled at just what had happened, they turned to the superior, supposedly all-knowing race for an explanation.

"Wolves," we told them. "The wolves have caused this. We'll go to work with poison and airplanes and buckshot and everything will soon be all right."

In Canada's Northwest Territory the first white men who penetrated the fringes of the Barrens and made contact with the Inland Eskimos were fur traders. Their attempts to make trappers out of hunters were no more designed for the benefit of the Eskimos than were the Alaskan attempts to make herdsmen out of them. And no more successful. For just a few seasons these people gave up their caribou hunting and brought fox pelts down to the trading posts to exchange for supplies and rifles and cartridges. Then the price of fox fur dropped and the northernmost posts were abandoned. After a few winters of starving the Eskimos went back to caribou hunting with a vengeance, now equipped with modern rifles. There were a few years of plenty. Then the herds dwindled so that every winter was a starving winter. Until very recently the Canadian government had more or less pretended that the Inland Eskimos simply

243

didn't exist. Then the wretched condition of these people was given a good deal of publicity and the government was forced to act.

"Wolves," the authorities decided. "There are just too many wolves. We'll launch an all-out campaign to exterminate them. Then the Eskimos will have plenty to eat."

There are eight to ten thousand books published each year in this country and most of them find something wrong with the world, usually something that vast government expenditures would remedy quite nicely. The cause of the larger carnivora is most likely already a lost cause. The attitudes and practices that have characterized man's relationships with his fellow predators throughout all history are not going to be changed in the next few decades. But if we did wish to pull the wild hunters back from the brink of extinction, the first step would be to stop spending money, to save the millions that go for bounties and airplanes and poison. The next step would be to take a very small portion of this money and invest it in research and wildlife study, to find out what we were doing before we did anything else.

Instead, even on the Barrens where the wild things in no way conflict with civilization, we go on slaughtering wolves under the guise of conserving caribou. Just as we slaughter the pumas in mountain reaches we have no intention of using and claim we're conserving deer. Just as we slaughter the brown bears on little worthless Alaskan islands and insist we're conserving salmon. As unbelievable as it seems, in these areas where all forms of wildlife could exist without interfering with man in any way, far more animals have been killed off in the name of conservation than have been conserved.

Actually, the creatures in these regions would gradually recover from the damage we've done if we merely gave them a certain amount of protection and then left them alone. The caribou and the musk oxen would adapt themselves to the rifles we've placed in the hands of the Eskimos and learn to avoid man even at a distance, a lesson the wolves have already learned.

244

Nature is capable of healing such wounds, a process that takes place after fire or flood.

But this is something we feel we have to refuse to admit. No matter how obvious it becomes that most of our efforts at conservation have been only pretense, that even our honest efforts have been strictly trial and error and mostly error, we still have to assert our superiority. We are simply incapable of facing the fact that our fumbling attempts are inferior to Nature's own game-management program. Humility has never been a characteristic of men or wolves or bears or cats. Humility is reserved for the plant-eaters.

As far back as history is written, man has believed he was something more than an animal. He has searched tirelessly for a clear-cut distinction that would set him apart. Scientists have cautiously suggested that man was once an animal, that he became something more when he learned to develop tools rather than develop himself as animals did.

The pseudo-scientific belief that we descended from apes, a result of misreading Darwin, is every bit as fanciful as the American Indian's belief he descended from grizzly bears. No one knows what we were before we learned to make tools. But we certainly weren't the timid little grub-eating monkey-like creature so often described by imaginative anthropologists. We were a carnivore, a wild hunter, a pack-running creature similar in everything except appearance to today's wolf. We were so completely a predator that our desire to hunt has outlasted our need to hunt by many centuries.

Philosophers have never considered tool-making to be a complimentary-enough distinction between man and animal and have always been seeking a better answer. John Steinbeck, the only present-day philosopher who writes well enough to keep a man away from his hunting, once insisted that man is the only living thing that will suffer and die for a concept. But, with all due respect and admiration, John Steinbeck obviously never witnessed a lemming migration.

If we are really a completely different form of life than even

245

the higher mammals, then we have, in the next fifty years, a chance to reassure ourselves of this that will never come again. None of the tools we've developed or the things we've created with those tools is any real evidence of a special relationship with the Almighty. But here is an opportunity to prove conclusively that we're something greater than the wolf ... by not doing exactly what the wolf would do if he and not we had conquered the biotic checks designed to keep any one species from dominating the earth, by not exterminating competing predators. All of our cyanide and buckshot prove nothing more than the wolf's superior jaws and lungs prove when he runs down the smaller coyotes and foxes.

The only men who could conceivably perform the near-impossible task of saving the wolves, the bears and the big cats of North America from extinction are men who want to kill them.

No matter how conclusively naturalists prove that wolves have a place in the wild scheme of things, the poison and airplane-hunting campaigns will go on. No matter how many zoology professors demand that all Alaskan bear country be made into another Yellowstone Park, the bears will still be slaughtered and their home forests leveled and shipped to Japan for a quick profit. No matter how often wildlife studies indicate that our deer herds (which are rapidly becoming semi-domesticated) need more predation, bounties will still be paid for the hides of the few big cats who manage to escape the hired government trappers.

But if the 15 to 20 million hunters of this country were ever to rear up on their hind legs and start howling, the smugness would disappear very quickly from the faces of the politicians who are so fond of saying that the question of conservation has never yet influenced a major election. And, yachtsmen and piano players and golf players all having had their day, we might even someday have another man like Teddy Roosevelt in the White House.

But we've been tricked and sold out with monotonous regularity. We've been told that wolf extermination is being carried on for our benefit, that wolves must go so that we'll have caribou to hunt. (As if the simple cow-like caribou was any real trophy or, except for the transportation problem, any challenge to a hunter!) We've been told that puma extermination is going to preserve our deer hunting forever, in spite of the fact that very few men enter puma country while deer hunting. In the case of the bears it's been a little harder to trick us, for the bears, unlike the wolves and pumas, are presently considered extremely valuable game animals. But the exterminators have overcome this obstacle in a hundred devious ways. The rapidly dwindling numbers of our larger bears show this quite clearly.

No political party has ever championed conservation. No political party ever will until the outdoorsmen of this country make themselves heard as effectively as much smaller groups have been doing for years. And there is little indication that this will take place.

Far too many men who will willingly and eagerly spend thousands of dollars on an Alaskan bear-hunting trip will not spend a few minutes complaining to their representatives that Alaskan bears may soon be too few for hunting. As far as the wolves and big cats are concerned, they are usually not even considered game animals and have few defenders among hunters. Men who call themselves conservationists and organizations that call themselves conservation clubs have been as guilty as the exterminators in sending them down the one-way trail to oblivion.

These, then, are the North American wild hunters, the creatures who, in intelligence and social organization, most closely resemble man himself. These are the three families of larger carnivora: the family that has produced, in the dog, man's closest friend and, in the wolf, his most feared and hated enemy; the bear family, most powerful and deadly of all carnivora, the supreme trophy to the hunter; and the big cats, Nature's most highly-specialized and perfectly-developed physical specimens, perhaps the most beautiful of all wild animals.

If we no longer wish them to exist on this continent, we have only to keep our present policies toward them in force for a few more decades. But even modified by civilization, North America is a giant land. There is still room enough here. Free from bounties and poison and airplanes, preyed upon only by sportsmen using sporting methods, these creatures could survive for centuries, interfering in no way with civilization, keeping alive a form of recreation that is in itself a major industry, providing a badly-needed escape from the mounting pressures of a steel and concrete world.

BIBLIOGRAPHY AND
SELECTED REFERENCES

ANONYMOUS

1921. "Cleverest of All Animal Criminals." *Current Opinion.*
    March.

1921. "Widely Famous Custer Wolf Hits the Long, Long Trail."
    American Sheep Breeder and Wool Grower. March.

1921. "Custer Wolf." *Independent.* May 21.

1923. "Are Canadian Timber Wolves Man-killers?" *Literary
    Digest.* April 14.

1926. "History and Capture of Three Toes." *Dakota Farmer.*
    January 15.

1932. "Sanctuary for Brown Bears." *Nature Magazine.* January.

1932. "Brown and Grizzly Bears of Admiralty Should be Pro-
    tected." *Nature Magazine.* December.

1934. "Bears of Admiralty." *Nature Magazine.* January.

ASHLEY-MONTAGU, M. F.

1943. (Review) "Wolf-children and Feral Man." J. A. L. Singh
    and Robert Zingg. 1942. Harper's. *American Anthro-
    pologist.* July.

BURT, WILLIAM H.

1948. *The Mammals of Michigan.* University of Michigan Press.

CAHALANE, VICTOR H.

1954. *Mammals of North America.* MacMillan.

CAMP, RAYMOND R.

1954. *The Hunter's Encyclopedia.* Stackpole.

DUFRESNE, FRANK

1941. "Brown Danger." *Colliers.* June 28.

1954. "Will They Attack?" *Field and Stream.* February.

ELWELL, NISKA
  1956. "Beyond the Three-mile Limit." *Field and Stream.* May.

FERGUSON, G. W.
  1914. "Cougar vs. Grizzly." *Field and Stream.* October.

FORD, COREY
  1955. "Biggest Bear on Earth." *Saturday Evening Post.* November 12.

GABRIELSON, IRA N.
  1951. "Crisis for Alaskan Wildlife." *Audubon Magazine.* November.

GESELL, ARNOLD
  1941. "Wolf Child and Human Child." *Methuen.*

GILLHAM, C. E.
  1956. "Grizzly Death." *Sports Afield.* December.

GRANGER, W. O.
  1922. "End of the Outlaw Wolf." *Wallace's Farmer.* December 8.

HIBBEN, FRANK
  1948. *Hunting American Lions.* Crowell.
  1950. *Hunting American Bears.* Lippincott.

HOLZWORTH, JOHN MICHAEL
  1930. *Wild Grizzlies of Alaska.* G. P. Putnam's Sons.

McCRACKEN, HAROLD
  1955. *The Beast That Walks Like Man.* Hanover House.

MILLS, ENOS ABIJAH
  1919. *The Grizzly, Our Greatest Wild Animal.* Houghton Mifflin.

NEFF, E. D.
  1951. "Can We Save the Gray Wolf?" *Natural History.* November.

ORMSBEE, C. O.
  1918. "Trapping the Timber Wolf." *Country Gentlemen.* November 2.

PACK, A. N.
  1935. "Admiralty's Bears." *Nature's Magazine.* August.

REARDON, J.
    1955. "Shy Killer." *Outdoor Life*. October.
    1955. "Bears in the Air." *Outdoor Life*. November.

SETON, ERNEST THOMPSON
    1898. *Wild Animals I Have Known*. Charles Scribner's Sons.
    1900. *The Biography of a Grizzly*. Century.
    1909. *Life Histories of Northern Animals*. Charles Scribner's Sons.
    1929. *Lives of Game Animals*. Vol. 1, Vol. 2. Doubleday, Doran and Co.
    1937. *Great Historic Animals, Mainly about Wolves*. Charles Scribner's Sons.
    1942. "Lobo, King of the Currumpaw." *Reader's Digest*. November.

SIEMEL, SASHA
    1953. *Tigrero!* Prentice-Hall.

SINGH, J. A. L. and ZINGG, R. M.
    1942. *Wolf-children and Feral Man*. Harper's.

STEVENS, M. F. S.
    1943. *Meet Mr. Grizzly*. University of New Mexico Press.

STREEVER, FRED
    1948. *American Trail Hounds*. A. S. Barnes and Co.

WHITE, STEWART E.
    1930. "An Emergency Is Declared to Exist!" *Saturday Evening Post*. April 12.
    1930. "Alaska Bears." *Saturday Evening Post*. June 7.
    1931. "Grizzlies Again." *Saturday Evening Post*. February 21.

WHITLOCK, S. C.
    1950. "The Black Bear as a Predator of Man." *Journal of Mammalogy*. May.

WHITMORE, O. S.
    1909. "Treed by Wolves." *Outing*. March.

WILSON, R. H.
    1955. "Night of Cruel Cold." *Outdoor Life*. December.

WRIGHT, WILLIAM H.
    1909. *The Grizzly Bear*. Charles Scribner's Sons.
    1910. *The Black Bear*. Charles Scribner's Sons.

YOUNG, STANLEY P.
1930. *Hints on Coyote and Wolf Trapping.* U. S. Agricultural Leaflet 59:1-8.

YOUNG, STANLEY P. and GOLDMAN, EDWARD A.
1944. *The Wolves of North America.* American Wildlife Institute.
1946. *The Puma, Mysterious American Cat.* American Wildlife Institute.